Small Space Style

Small Space Style

Emma Scattergood

WARD LOCK

A WARD LOCK BOOK

First published in the UK 1997
by Ward Lock
Wellington House
125 Strand
London
WC2R 0BB

A Cassell Imprint
First published in paperback 1999
Copyright © 1997 Emma Scattergood

Distributed in the United States
by Sterling Publishing Co., Inc.
387 Park Avenue South, New York,
NY 10016–8810

A British Library Cataloguing in
Publication Data block for this book
may be obtained from the British
Library

ISBN 0 7063 7822 9

Designed and typeset by Jeffery Design
Illustrations by Amanda Patton
Printed and bound by South China
Printing Co. Ltd., Hong Kong

Contents

Introduction

If you live in a small apartment and the bedroom is part of your living space, it may be possible to conceal the bed by using a fold-away design. Make sure that the furniture in front of the cupboard is light so that it can be moved to one side at night, and, if possible, choose pieces that can be put to good use as bedside tables or somewhere to drape your clothes.

Who hasn't, at one time or another, longed for a spare bedroom, for more storage space or for a larger kitchen? Extra space at home is something that most of us dream of, although it is true to say that however much living space we have, it's not long before it becomes cluttered and begins to feel inadequate for our needs. Building an extension or moving home to gain more space are usually expensive or impracticable options, so most of us just struggle on, dissatisfied with our lot.

Stop right there! Now is the time to take control of the situation. All that is needed to transform your home – and your lifestyle – is an ability to take a fresh look at your living space and reassess its potential. With the right approach, even the smallest of living areas can be made to look and feel twice as spacious – it's just a matter of doing some serious planning and adopting a few tricks of the trade!

With the help of this book you will learn

how to get the most out of a small or awkward space and to make it appear larger than it really is. You will find that it is possible to make your small spaces work hard for you, offering you practical solutions to the problems arising from lack of space while presenting a truly stylish finish, too.

There are chapters focusing on every room in the home (including the hall and landing), offering tips and suggestions on how to maximize their potential, decorate them successfully and add extra storage space. There are sections on lighting small rooms, choosing the right furniture and dressing windows to best effect – there is even a whole chapter dedicated to colour and how you can use it to create the mood and the look that you want. The first and final chapters concentrate on planning and putting together your decorative scheme in the manner of a professional interior designer so that you can be certain that, with a little care, you will achieve a truly expert look.

It is often the spaces that offer the greatest challenge that result in the most successful interiors, so, rather than viewing your lack of space as a problem, see it as an opportunity to put your newly found skills to the test. With the help of *Small Space Style* you are sure to succeed!

Using unpatterned, pale colours across a one-roomed apartment makes it possible to create a greater impression of space than there actually is. Grouping the furniture into individual 'room sets' and creating visual 'divides' within the room, with the banister rail, lighting and the foot of the bed, help to make the scheme more successful.

Just because your space is limited does not mean that you have to hide away all your clutter and treasures. You may not have much wall space for displaying a collection, but you may be able to revamp an old wardrobe or cupboard to create an interesting and attractive focal point.

1 Planning and preparation

The careful use of lighting, glass and a harmonious colour scheme will help to create a serene, spacious look. Painting the alcove units the same colour as the walls and fitting them with glass shelves creates a sleek, unobtrusive effect, but the accessories play an essential part in preventing the overall effect from being rather flat and uninteresting.

Don't be put off by the rather boring prospect of preparation and planning. Although it sounds uninspiring and dull, this is the most important part of redesigning your living space, and the time and energy you put into this stage could make or break the effect of your new scheme.

It is very tempting to dive straight in with a paintbrush or rush out to the shops and splash out on some brand new furniture, but try to restrain yourself – for a while at least. If you want to get the best possible results, you should go about decorating your home in the same way as a professional interior designer, and that means taking time to make sure that what you do is right for the room and the people using it. If you had only been thinking about applying a coat of fresh paint and perhaps moving around the three-piece suite, this may all seem rather unnecessary, but taking this approach will help you get impressive results and possibly even save you from decorating yet again in just a few months' time.

Be professional

Imagine that, instead of tackling it yourself, you have decided to spend your money on hiring the services of a professional interior designer to give your home a new look. You would be rather worried if he or she took a quick look at a room then reached for a paint pot! You would expect a professional to approach the task by talking through what you want from the room, how it could be made to work better for you and how to make it look more stylish – and then to put together an accurate picture of the ways in which the room could be changed to meet your needs. So, if you are serious about redesigning your home (and you must be, or you would not have picked up this book), you should go about it in the same way a professional would, and that means following the guidelines suggested here. It's a foolproof way of getting excellent results!

Gather information

You want your home to look wonderful, but it needs to be practical too. Small homes needn't be any less stylish than more spacious ones, but you do have to work a bit harder to make sure that they are practical living spaces. Everything in the home has got to work for you as well as look good, or you won't enjoy spending time in it any more than you do now.

In order to gather an accurate picture of how each room can be made a useful yet comfortable space, you need to ask yourself (and anyone else who lives there) questions about how you want or need to use the room. You must be honest with yourself. It is no good planning a home around an idealized or unrealistic lifestyle. Professionals may refer to this stage as 'taking the brief' and would come with a notebook and tape measure in order to do the job properly and get a complete picture. Here are some suggestions about the kind of questions you should be asking yourself at this stage.

For every room

Whether you are drawing up plans for a one- or two-roomed apartment or for a whole house, there are some general questions that you need to consider before you even reach for a colour chart.

What is the budget?

The most important question of all is 'how much money can I spend?' Before you start dreaming of new furniture, you need to establish a maximum figure for your expenditure on each room, then take off about 10 per cent to keep aside for unforeseen items. Once you start working, unexpected expenses will inevitably arise.

Once you have set yourself a total figure, ask yourself what your priorities are, and break down the budget accordingly. In other words, if you feel faint at the prospect of spending more than £500 on new curtains, make a note of that now. It will help you control the expenditure when you come across a fabric that you would die for but that would cost £800 to be made up. Next, you can allocate the remaining money to the other items you need. Don't feel that this part of the budget planning is cast in stone, however. You can always cast caution to the wind and buy the expensive curtains, just as long as you are aware that, as a result, you will have to be more frugal in other areas and perhaps spend less on your floor covering or furniture. It's up to you to juggle the budget according to your own priorities.

Once you start window shopping for furniture and furnishings, keep a note of the price of anything you consider buying and, before you spend any money, add it all up.

It's the best way of being sure that you keep within your means. You may want to start keeping a notebook for all the above reminders and plans. A small notebook that you can take with you when you are shopping is useful, but you will need to combine it with a folder that is large enough to hold the brochures, invoices and so on that you are sure to accumulate. Keep this information together because it will be a useful reference if you need to check any details in the future and it may even be an interesting memento, too!

Who will be using the room?

A room is successful only if it meets the requirements of everyone who uses it on a regular basis – and when space is short, every inch counts. Your list of people to consider should include your pets, especially dogs, as their lifestyle will make an impact on your furnishings too!

You need to consider if different people use the same room for different activities – reading and watching television, for example, or eating and doing homework. Do you need to think about creating quiet corners or places where family members can keep personal possessions, and so on?

What are the best and worst points?

Can you remember your impression of the room on the day you moved in? Are there any particularly attractive features and what did you immediately dislike? Thinking along these lines is likely to give you your most accurate picture of the room's good and bad points. Other aspects will have become apparent if you have lived in the space for a while, so make a note of those, too – even if you're not sure how you would set about tackling them at this stage.

Don't worry if your list of 'dislikes' is twice the length of your 'likes' – that is often the

Do not forget the space you have above your head – it could be valuable! Free-standing furniture does not offer the same opportunities for overhead storage as custom-made schemes, when even the gap above the door can be put to good use. If you do not like the open-plan look, soften it with a curtain or blind front or with fitted cupboard doors.

way with small, awkward rooms. With a little planning and care, it is possible to transform even the ugliest of features into something that is less noticeable – even if you cannot make it beautiful!

What kind of floor is there?

Your choice of floor coverings will be restricted if the floor is not a solid one (i.e., not concrete), especially if you are thinking about installing heavy floor finishes, such as ceramic tiles or marble.

Do you have enough storage space?

Asking yourself if you have enough storage space will almost certainly produce the answer 'no'. The problem with small-space living is that it makes enormous demands on a small area, and keeping even just the day-to-day clutter tidied away can be difficult. Consider early on how you might make best use of the space in the room to include plenty of storage options that do not appear too obtrusive.

What elements will be staying?

In addition to noting any elements that you do not want or cannot change, note anything that you are prepared to be more flexible with. It is unlikely that you will be starting completely from scratch. You may have to work around an existing carpet, sofa or curtains, but this can actually be an advantage, as it gives you something to use as a starting point, especially when it comes to putting together a colour scheme.

Is there any natural light?

Small rooms need to be tackled with especial care if they do not receive much light. Are there any ways in which you might improve the light in the room, such as by adding another window? These are decisions that should be made now – not after you've put up the wallpaper.

Use a compass to check which way the window faces. North- and east-facing rooms receive less direct sunlight than south- and west-facing rooms, so they will appear darker and colder. If you want to create as much of an impression of light as possible you will need to take this into account when you plan your colour scheme. However, if you feel that increasing the room's natural light is going to be too difficult or too expensive, you could try emphasizing the room's darker, more dramatic nature instead (see Chapter 2 on colour).

Is the lighting and socket supply adequate?

You need to consider the lighting and electricity socket schemes at any early point in the planning stage. Putting in sockets and running cables up walls is going to ruin any decorating scheme. Always think about how your needs might change in the future and incorporate enough sockets to give the flexibility to introduce new equipment or even to move the furniture around. In a child's room especially the number of electrically run gadgets is likely to increase substantially as time goes by, and introducing additional sockets now will avoid problems later.

Is the heating adequate?

Adding or moving radiators and opening up fireplaces are also disruptive jobs and need to be done before any decoration starts.

How do you use the room?

This is the crucial question and the one that will determine everything, from the colours you use to decorate it (so that you create the right atmosphere) to the type of furniture you choose and how you position it (to allow your family traffic to circulate freely around the room). Look at the individual room checklists below for further pointers.

Bedroom

■ Is there room to have a sink installed? Estate agents claim that an *en suite* bathroom is one investment that will certainly make your home more sellable if not more valuable. That aside, a sink in the bedroom will reduce the pressure on the bathroom first thing in the morning.

■ Does someone put on make-up here?

■ Are there enough mirrors in the room?

■ What sort of volume of clothes do you need to store here? Are they mostly suits or do you also need full-length hanging space? Would free-standing or fitted wardrobes be more suitable?

■ Do you have to store suitcases or sports equipment in the bedroom? Where will you put them? Would overhead cupboards solve this problem?

■ Do you watch television in bed? If so, do you have a power point in the right place. If reception is bad, do you need to consider having an aerial socket added?

■ Is the room also a work space? You will need extra storage space and a table. Perhaps you could find a piece of furniture that could act as both desk and dressing-table.

■ Is the room also to be a living room? If so, a seating and living area will be as important as the sleeping and dressing facilities.

Look out for small-scale pieces of furniture to suit your small rooms. You could even have a bed specially adapted or made for the space you have available. Here, by continuing the floral pattern from the bed, over the bedside table and onto the chair, the overall look has been brought together to make the room seem less bitty and cluttered.

Living room

■ How many people sit and read here at any one time? You will need to have enough chairs with adequate lighting.

■ Does anyone like to stretch out and doze in this room? The lighting will need to be flexible to allow them to do so and you will need a comfortable sofa.

■ Is the living room also going to be used as a study? Consider where your desk would be best positioned for the light and if there is a point for the phone line. Do you need to have additional electric sockets for a computer? Will you need shelving space for books and papers?

■ Is it to be a formal living room or more of a family room? The style of decoration and furnishing will be more practical in a family room than in a room that is used by just one or two people.

■ Do you need to incorporate storage space for toys?

■ Will children be playing in here? If so, safety will need to be considered carefully. Remember to guard against furniture that has sharp corners, and make sure that flexes do not trail and that fires are provided with serviceable guards.

■ Is the hi-fi going to be installed in here? Perhaps you will want to have an extra set of

The pale colours make the walls of this living room appear to recede, and the neutral frames and mounts for the pictures hanging on the walls and the corner cupboard do not interrupt this effect. A bold picture, painted in fiery colours, will immediately draw the eye to the wall and make it appear to advance into the room, so be careful with your choice of pictures and accessories if you want to maintain the impression of space created by the pale walls.

Most books require comparatively shallow shelves, so it is possible to provide storage for plenty of books without losing much living space, and a specially built unit can save valuable inches. A standard dresser would have been rather bulky in this small room, but the same effect has been achieved within less space. If you need to incorporate an eating area into your kitchen space, homely touches, such as table lamps and bookshelves, will help create an identifiably separate area.

speakers in here and have the system based in another room, such as the dining room or kitchen. The extension work is best done before you start decorating, and you need to plan where you will house CDs, tapes or records.

■ Where can the TV be positioned so that it can be seen from most angles yet not be in the light? Is there an appropriately sited aerial socket?

■ Does anyone want to pursue a particular hobby in this room? Will they need special facilities, such as lighting or a table, to do so comfortably?

■ Do you have a collection of some kind that will be displayed? Consider how that can be done to best effect. Do you need to arrange special lighting or shelving for it?

■ Is there an open fireplace? Will it be useful to you as a working fireplace, or could it be put to better use if a gas fire were added or the chimney area were used for something else?

■ Would a coffee table be useful? If there is space, a low table can be a convenient place to store magazines and to play games as well as to put coffee cups.

■ Is the room also going to be your dining area? Is there space for a permanent dining area, and, if so, where will be the best place for a table and chairs? Will you need to keep dining equipment stored elsewhere or in this room?

Kitchen

■ Who cooks most? Make sure that whoever spends most time in the kitchen is the person who is most involved in the planning process.

■ Do you cook alone or as a couple? The amount of space you need will vary accordingly.

■ How often do you shop? Do you need large food storage areas and space for a large fridge-freezer or do you stock up on a daily basis?

■ What are your eating and cooking habits? Do you live on convenience foods, which can go into the microwave, or do you prepare elaborate meals regularly? Your lifestyle will dictate the type of kitchen you need.

■ How large is your batterie de cuisine? Consider where and how it would be best stored.

■ If you do not have a separate dining room and if your living room is too small for a separate dining area, will you eat in the kitchen? Do you need a breakfast bar for quick snacks or have you got to incorporate a proper dining area?

■ Do you use a lot of labour-saving gadgets? They will all need storage space (usually on a worktop near at hand) and enough sockets.

Where the kitchen leads straight into the living area, look at ways of softening the divide between the two areas. Choose a colour that is not out of place in either setting and make the fittings work for both 'rooms'. A worktop could offer practical kitchen storage space on one side, and be furnished with shelves for books or ornaments on the other. Here a picture and a vase of flowers give a homely look to the living side.

Painting a low ceiling in a cool, pale colour will make it appear less obtrusive, but rather than allowing a lower than average ceiling to defeat you, why not make it work to your advantage and use it to hang shelves and other accessories. Taking the window dressings right up to the ceiling not only helps to create the impression of extra height but also means that you will not obscure any of the natural light from the windows.

A bathroom is the ideal place to emphasize, rather than attempt to detract from, cramped proportions. The occupant has plenty to look at, and the room becomes an entertaining place to enjoy a soak. The cramped bathing facilities on board ship must have been the inspiration for this tiny room.

Bathroom

■ Do you prefer quick, invigorating showers or long, hot soaks in a tub? Your answer will dictate your choice of suite and fittings.

■ Do you have children who will want to use the facilities as independently as possible? You will need to think about incorporating steps to the basin and toilet, easy-to-use toilet flush and tap facilities and even a bath with low sides.

■ Do you keep a laundry basket in the bathroom? You may want to find a way of incorporating such storage as neatly as possible.

■ Do you air clothes in here? Is there room for an airing cupboard or a hanging clothes airer?

■ Are there any elderly people in the home who have special needs, such as easy-to-turn taps, a non-slip bath and grips at the sides of the bath?

■ Do you need to replace the whole suite or could you give it a new look with the help of new bath panels and tiles?

■ Is the basin large enough for your needs?

■ Do you want a practical, functional room or are you yearning for a softer, luxurious finish?

■ Do you live in an area that has hard or soft water? Lime-scale builds up quickly in hard water areas and you should be aware of this when you choose your tiles and fittings.

Hall and landing

■ Do you have a lot of dirty feet regularly coming through the hallway? If you have pets or children, the hallway is going to have to withstand more dirt and mess than in an average home as will any living space that opens onto a grassy rather than a paved area.

■ Do you have a lot of mail delivered? You may want somewhere to place it for sorting and now is the time to consider having a mail box fixed to the front door.

■ Do you have a lot of heavy coats in regular use? If bedroom storage is limited, should you be thinking about creating a hanging area in the hall?

■ Do you often leave messages for other occupants? The hall is a very good site for a message board.

■ Is the telephone point in the hallway? If so, you will want somewhere to store directories or write notes. Do you need to consider having a small writing ledge and folding chair nearby?

■ Does anyone in the home tend to get up in the night a lot? You may want to think about subdued night lighting, perhaps controlled by a timer or a light-sensitive switch.

■ Consider your security. The front door may be the easiest access point for potential burglars. Think about the locks and security devices on the front door and, if you have a house, you might want to assess the need for security lighting.

■ Are you likely to convert a loft space in the future? If so, consider now what sort of access you would have to the loft and where the stairs would be sited.

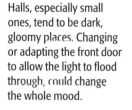

Halls, especially small ones, tend to be dark, gloomy places. Changing or adapting the front door to allow the light to flood through, could change the whole mood.

Keeping a child's bedroom simply decorated and considering the storage space carefully, mean that it is possible to make even a small room adapt to your child's changing needs over the years.

Children's room

The questions you will need to ask yourself will vary tremendously according to the age of your child or children, but the following will give you some ideas for the kinds of areas you need to include in your preliminary planning.

■ Are you thinking about having any more children? If so, will they share this bedroom?

■ Will this room also need to be a playroom? Or is that going to be sited elsewhere?

■ Will you want to use this room as a focus for all your baby's activities, from feeding and changing through to bathing, in much the same way as most traditional nurseries were used? Alternatively, will it be nothing more than a sleeping space to begin with?

■ Has your child already developed special interests or collections? School children in particular will have hobbies that require space to accommodate them.

Planning on paper

Once you have identified your basic requirements, you need to work out the best way of incorporating these into your small space. This is the difficult part, but it can also be fun, provided you do it on paper first. This enables you to get an accurate view of how you can divide up your living space and what pieces of furniture will fit where, without your actually having to move pieces of furniture until you find the layout you like. It also means that you can evaluate the space available before you buy any furniture.

How to do it

Don't panic. You do not need to be artistic or even any good at drawing to prepare a useful plan. First, you need to measure your complete floor area accurately. This isn't just a matter of finding out how wide and long it is (or rather, how short and narrow it is!) You also need to note the width of the door, the length of every radiator, the position of the window and so on. Begin by drawing a rough sketch of the shape of your floor space and mark on it the measurements that you make. Double check the accuracy of your measuring

Once you have gathered all the measurements of the room, draw a scaled floor plan on squared paper. A scale of 1:20 or 1:25 should be sufficient of fit the room onto a sheet of A4 (11¾×8¼in). Sketch out the lines for the walls before adding the positions of windows, radiators, doors and so on and add the measurements for each feature.

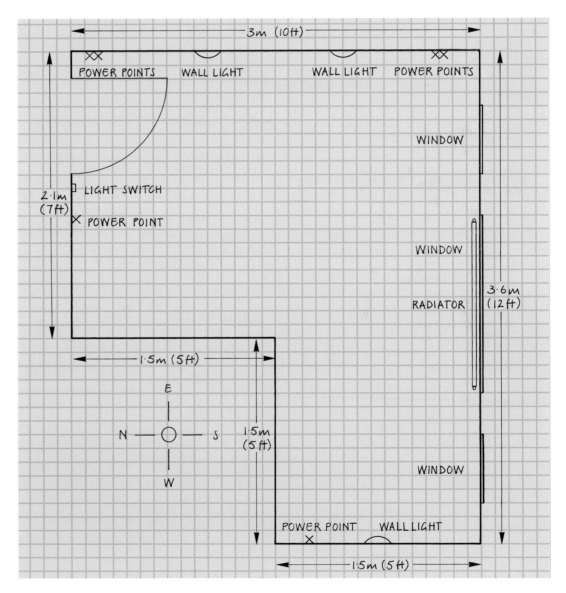

by adding up the individual smaller measurements, such as corner to window, window to radiator, and radiator to corner, to see if they add up to the one measurement from corner to corner. If there are any built-in cupboards, measure their depth, and make a note of how far the existing door comes into the room when it is opened.

While you are busy with your tape measure and notebook, it is worth making notes of other measurements too, such as the size of your windows, the drop from sill to floor and so on, as you will need them in the future. In fact, the more measurements you take at this stage and have to hand whenever you go shopping, the better – you might be able to snap up a few sale bargains as a result.

The next task is to transform your sketch into a scaled drawing by transferring all the measurements onto squared paper. You will need to use a scale that allows you to fit your plan comfortably onto a sheet of A4 ($11^3/4 \times 8^1/4$in) or A3 ($16^1/2 \times 11^3/4$in) – a scale of 1:20 is normally sufficient – and use a ruler for accuracy. Do it with a pencil first until you are sure you've got it right, and ink in the lines afterwards if you want to. Once you are happy with the floor plan, mark on it the positions of the

What you need to make your plans

- ☐ Notebook and pen
- ☐ Steel tape measure
- ☐ Two or more sheets of squared paper (at least A4/$11^3/4 \times 8^1/4$in)
- ☐ Ruler (preferably a scale ruler)
- ☐ Pencil
- ☐ Fine black pen
- ☐ Tracing paper
- ☐ Scissors

power points, radiators and TV socket. Don't forget to indicate the direction the doors open and where the window is. You should also make a note of which way the room faces (south, north and so on) so that you remember what sort of light the room receives. In addition, mark the major measurements on the plan, so that you can see at a glance how much room you have in a particular corner. If you make a note of both metric and imperial measurements, the plan will be more instantly useful wherever you shop. You may even want to calculate how many square metres or square feet of floor space you have and mark that on the plan, too, so that the information is readily to hand when you come to think about the floor covering.

Now measure any pieces of furniture that you know are definitely staying in the room. You do not need to know their height, only their width and depth (you could keep a note of the height too – it may prove useful later). Convert these dimensions to the same scale as your plan and cut them out of squared paper. Label each little cut-out 'sofa', 'bed' and so on, so that you do not confuse your bed with the dining table, and as a double check you should write the dimensions on them as well. If you are planning to buy a new piece of furniture and do not yet know how big it will be, look through a few catalogues. You will soon get an idea of the average sizes of, say, a two- or three-seater sofa and the sort of table you want, and you can use these as a rough guide even if you don't find a design you will actually want to buy.

Now you can use your floor plan and the pieces of cut-out 'furniture' to play around with the arrangement of the room until you achieve the perfect compromise of style and practicality. (Read the chapter appropriate to the room you are redesigning first, to help you do this.) Once you are happy with the plan, or even just a part of it, trace it,

Sketching each wall or 'elevation' in a room will allow you to experiment with the different schemes you are considering and assess how they will look *in situ*. If you create a master drawing to scale in black ink, similar to those illustrated here, you can use tracing paper to show different elements, placing them on top of each other and removing them until you are happy with the overall result.

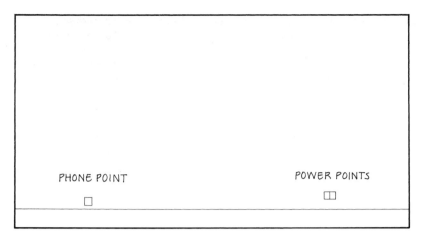

PHONE POINT

POWER POINTS

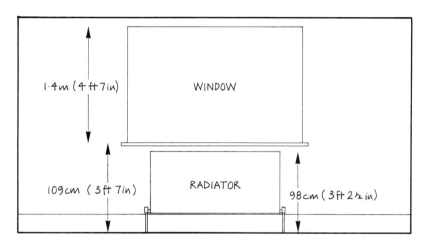

1·4m (4 ft 7in)

WINDOW

109cm (3ft 7in)

RADIATOR

98cm (3ft 2½ in)

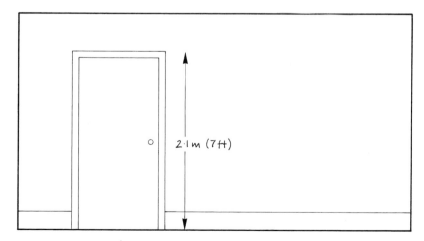

2·1 m (7ft)

complete with the positioned furniture, onto tracing paper and put it to one side. Doing this allows you to juggle around with several ideas, without losing track of arrangements you have already tried. This technique is particularly useful when you are planning a small room as you can see exactly how much you can fit into a confined space and judge if it would work practically.

Making an elevation sketch

If you want to take your planning one step further, you could produce some elevation sketches. These are essentially a drawing of each wall in the room that, if done to scale, can give you an accurate impression of how the finished room will look. Use the measurements you have taken to draw a scaled diagram of each wall area, including architectural and fixed details, such as fireplaces, windows, radiators, skirting boards, coving and so on. Use a ruler so that the finished drawing resembles a plan rather than an artist's sketch. Now, on tracing paper, you can experiment with how additions such as different curtain styles, mirrors, shelving, wall lights and so on will look *in situ*. Use a different piece of tracing paper for every new feature so that you can build up layers of tracings to produce the final look while being able to omit or add different elements. You can even introduce colour and design to the tracing paper sketches with inks or crayons.

By now you will have built up a very detailed picture of the room you are designing, which, when it is combined with the other information you have gathered, will set you on course for making a truly practical and stylish small space!

2 Colour for small spaces

A colour wheel

An understanding of colour is a powerful weapon to have on your side when you are faced with making the most of a small living area. Colour can completely transform the look of a room and even its mood. The right colour combinations can make a room appear larger, warmer and more exciting or cooler and more restful. The wrong combinations can, of course, create the opposite effects.

Unfortunately, too many of us are rather scared of colour and worried that we will make an expensive mistake, so we tend to stick to white, magnolia or, at best, pastel shades in every room in the home. There is no excuse for this. Not only are the style gurus dictating that we strike a little bolder with our brushes, but the shops are packed with exciting ranges of glorious paint colours. More important than this however, is the simple fact that *anyone* can learn to use colour effectively – it's just a matter of following a few straightforward guidelines.

Colour theory

Don't be put off by the word 'theory' – the basic principles of colour are not technical or difficult to digest. A useful guide to the basis of colour is the colour wheel, which is created by taking the primary colours (red, blue and yellow), and mixing any two of them in equal proportions to produce the secondary colours (violet, green and orange). The secondary colours lie on the colour wheel between the two colours that have been mixed to create them. The wheel is expanded even further by mixing any two secondary colours together to make tertiary colours – and so on. Complementary colours are those that lie opposite each other on the wheel – blue and orange, for example – and related colours are those that sit next to each other – deep yellow and orange, for example. The wheel can be made even more detailed by dividing each individual segment of colour into further sections to show the effect of adding different amounts of white to that colour.

But what has all this got to do with how you decorate your bedroom? The answer is that you can use the finished colour wheel to help decide on your colour scheme and to give you confidence in your colour combinations. In other words, by looking at the wheel you can decide which complementary colour would make an appropriate contrast with your orange carpet (blue, for example) or which related colour would work equally well with your yellow kitchen.

If you like a coordinated, harmonious

A traditional interior doesn't always demand a traditional colour scheme. The warm sunlight flooding in from this south-facing window is the ideal complement to an unusual but effective combination of colours.

Screens of colour are the perfect way of breaking up one-room apartments into separate areas. Here the colours chosen for the screens and sofa may have been inspired by the striking picture. A large picture works best in a room where there is the space to stand back and appreciate it and where it does not dominate the setting entirely. Groups of smaller pictures are often more appropriate for less spacious rooms.

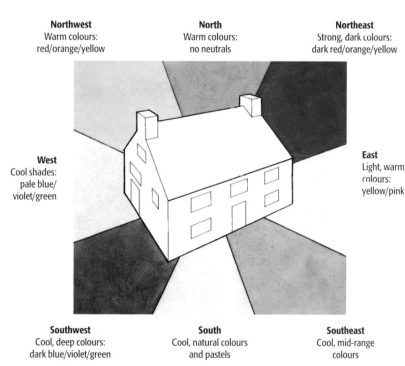

Northwest
Warm colours:
red/orange/yellow

North
Warm colours:
no neutrals

Northeast
Strong, dark colours:
dark red/orange/yellow

West
Cool shades:
pale blue/
violet/green

East
Light, warm
colours:
yellow/pink

Southwest
Cool, deep colours:
dark blue/violet/green

South
Cool, natural colours
and pastels

Southeast
Cool, mid-range
colours

The type of light a room receives will affect the colours in the room and the success of your scheme. Sunlight from the south or west, for example, casts a warm glow and allows you to create a welcoming scheme with cool colours and pastels. Rooms that face north or east receive a colder light and need to be warmed by colours from the opposite side of the colour wheel.

look, you can play safe by adopting a colour scheme that uses related colours (those that lie next to each other on the wheel). Some of the most sophisticated schemes are created using only the various shades and tints of just one colour. If you feel that you would like a bit more contrast and excitement, however, adding an accent colour from the opposite or complementary side of the wheel will bring your scheme to life. Using equal amounts of two contrasting colours in the same room is generally to be avoided unless you want a truly dramatic effect!

Aspect

An awareness of the effects of certain colours can be put to good use if it is combined with a knowledge of the way your home faces and the kind of light each room receives. Different colours reflect light in different ways, so your decoration is inevitably affected by the type of light that enters the room. Light from the north and east is colder looking than that from the south and west so, as a general guide, it is best to use warm colours in north- and east-facing rooms and cool colours in south- and west-facing rooms.

Blue is a receding rather than an advancing colour, so it is a good choice for a small room. Only use it in a kitchen that receives warm light, however, or the effect could be too cold.

The psychology of colour

The colour wheel can help your decision-making in another important respect – creating an atmosphere. View the colour wheel as if it were cut in two, into a warm half and a cool half. Colours in the yellow/red half make up the warm colours of the wheel, while the blue/green half consists of the cooler colours. By opting for colours from a particular side of the wheel you immediately make an impact on the atmosphere of that room. No one needs a psychologist to explain that colours can play tricks on the mind. Decorate any room in intense cool colours and you'll create a space that is bright, refreshing and cheering. Opt for their more subdued tints and the result will be peaceful, calming and even formal. A room decorated in reds, oranges and warm yellows however will soon make people feel warm and relaxed.

Individual colours also have certain associations, which make them particularly appropriate for certain rooms, whatever their size or limitations.

Blue

Renowned for being a calming, peaceful colour, blue is a good choice for a bathroom (especially when it verges towards aqua or turquoise) or a bedroom. Do be careful, however, that the room receives plenty of warm sunlight to prevent the overall effect from being too cold (see page 29).

Yellow

Always associated with sunshine and sunny days, yellow is invariably cheerful and welcoming, making it a good choice for a kitchen or breakfast room, or even a hallway and landing. Using a bold colour such as warm yellow on the walls can be especially successful if you have little in the way of interesting furniture or accessories, because it creates a more united look and provides a good backdrop for the simplest of objects.

Green

In its deeper, richer shades green is reminiscent of a traditional library, and it works well when it is combined with a similarly rich red. In small spaces, however, the effect will be dark and dramatic, so be careful, and use it only if you want to emphasize the room's cosiness.

In its cooler, lighter tints, green is bright and refreshing. If you have a garden or a balcony, light greens are ideal for kitchens that open to the outdoors. Remember to use a shade of green that is warmed up with a tint of yellow or it will look too cold and even clinical.

Pink

Romantic and warm, pink is an ideal choice for a bedroom, whether you choose its most delicately subtle tones or a wild, vivid shade. However, pink can be such a warm, cheerful colour that it would suit any room, so do not feel that it must be used only in a bedroom. Pale pink always looks fresh, and never more so than when it is combined with touches of green for a country garden look.

Violet or indigo

The richest shades of indigo can be stunning. A luxurious-looking colour, it is reminiscent of the church and formal pageantry. Softened to a paler tint, it is, like blue, a calming, peaceful colour.

If your room receives a rather chilly light and is a little on the dark side, don't be afraid to go for a bold yellow, no matter how small the area. It will make a space instantly warmer and more welcoming.

One of the conundrums of one-room living is how to choose a colour that will suit all the separate functions of the available space. The answer is to ignore convention and be bold. Pink can work in a kitchen so you can have a romantic bedroom and a sugar and spice kitchen if that is what you want.

Red is said to stimulate the appetite, and it will make a dining area appear cosy and warm, which is perfect for a small dining room. If your dining area forms part of an open-plan living room, be cautious with red – it may be rather overpowering for a room where you will also want to relax, read and even study.

Red

In its most primary form, red is stimulating in the extreme and should be used with caution – unless, that is, you are decorating a room you want no one to linger in for long! Deeper, more subdued reds are associated with grander, older country houses, especially the dining room – maybe because red is also said to stimulate the appetite!

Orange

Not a colour for the shy or faint-hearted! Like red it should be used carefully in its most vibrant shades unless you are determined to make a bold, dramatic statement, but when it is softened to a terracotta or deep apricot tone it is a wonderfully warming and more relaxing colour, perfect for a chilly dining or a north-facing living room.

In a one-room apartment, or a dual-purpose room, use splashes of colour to create a separate look for one area. This is also a good way of introducing colour on a small scale if you are still rather cautious about making a bold statement. Here the main expanse of wall has been painted in a neutral colour, but one striking panel gives the kitchen area a look all of its own.

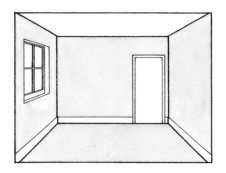

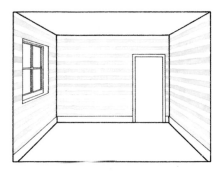

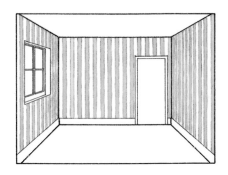

If you want to make a room look larger, choose pale or cool colours for the walls and floor covering.

If you would like to create an impression of greater space within a room, try decorating the walls with horizontal stripes. The walls immediately appear to be wider.

Vertical stripes will emphasize the height of a ceiling, taking the eye upwards and making the walls appear taller.

Warm (advancing) colours
Yellow
Yellow-orange
Orange
Orange-red
Red

Creating the illusion of space

When space is short you have two options – to emphasize a room's smallness or to fight back and try to create an impression of space. If your living area is small, you will probably immediately choose the second option, but you can use colour in different ways to achieve the look you want. Looking again at just a few principles of colour theory suggests ways in which we can use different colours and their shades and tones to make ceilings and walls recede or advance and thereby create an impression, albeit a false one, of having more or less space than there actually is.

So how is it done? Going back to the colour wheel once more, the shades from the warmer half of the colour wheel (warm yellow, orange and red) are also known as 'advancing' colours – that is, they appear closer to you than they actually are. This makes them an ideal choice if you want to draw attention to a particular wall or feature. Conversely, the cool colours on the opposite of the wheel (blue, green and violet) are known as 'receding' colours. Far from advancing towards you, they will appear to stay where they are or even recede.

Armed with that information, it becomes easier to distinguish which colours will work to make a room appear smaller and which

will help to create an impression of space. Remember, however, that this applies essentially to the true colours or hues. Once white is added to a colour in any quantity it becomes a tint (more commonly known as a pastel) and will lose the warmth it once possessed. Similarly, a darker shade or matt finish of any colour will lose its light-reflecting qualities. In other words, a dark, deep blue will not be as helpful in creating an impression of space in a room as a cool, true blue.

Some of the ways in which you can manipulate colour are summarized below.

Creating a general impression of space

■ Adopt a monochromatic colour scheme – that is, use various shades of one colour, such as white, cool blue or aqua green, to decorate and furnish the room throughout. It creates a feeling of airiness and the eye can pass over the room to its full extent more easily.

■ Fit a plain, wall-to-wall carpet in a cool colour and, ideally, continue the colour on walls. This makes it more difficult for the eye to distinguish the boundaries of the room.

■ Sustain the theme of cool colours when you choose your curtain fabric so that you don't ruin the effect as soon as your curtains are closed.

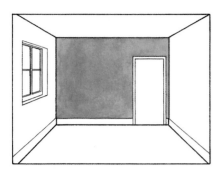

In a long, narrow room or corridor, painting the far wall in a warm colour will make it 'advance' and make the area as a whole appear to be better balanced.

Painting a ceiling in a darker colour than the walls, and extending the colour to the picture rail, makes the ceiling appear lower. A floor covering in a dark or warm colour will make the floor appear smaller, too.

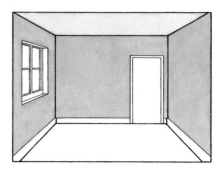

You can make the ceiling appear to be higher by painting it a lighter colour than the walls – although it doesn't have to be white.

Making a ceiling look higher

Try one or more of the following designer's tricks:

■ Paint the ceiling the same colour as the walls, or even a tone or two lighter, so that your eye continues onwards and upwards.

■ Decorate the ceiling in a colour that is lighter than your walls and use a light-reflecting material, such as Anaglypta wallpaper and/or a satin-finish paint.

■ Fix a painted picture rail or decorative shelf to draw the eye upwards.

■ Colour the ceiling to match the background of the wall covering to given an impression of continuity.

■ If your walls are to be decorated in a small-patterned print, continue the pattern up from the walls and over the ceiling. This works particularly well in giving rooms with sloping ceilings a country look.

■ Decorate the walls with vertical stripes, either in a wallpaper design or painted with a roller. Vertical stripes in an interior have the same effect as they do on someone's clothes! They encourage the eye to travel up and down, emphasizing the height rather than the width. Look at the illustrations on page 34 to see how the same room looks completely different when it is given a vertical emphasis and when it is given a horizontal emphasis.

Making a narrow room look wider

■ Increase the apparent width of the room by painting the skirting board to match the floor so that the floor appears to extend further than it actually does.

■ Put up a dado rail and paint the lower half of the wall under the dado and the skirting board the same colour as the floor (ideally a cooler colour) for a more marked effect.

■ Decorate the closer walls in receding colours and use warmer, deeper shades on the end walls to create a greater sense of balance in the room. If there are windows at one end of the room, use warm, deep coloured curtain fabric and hang full-length curtains to create the same effect when the curtains are closed.

■ Use a bold horizontal pattern, such as stripes, to emphasize the width of the two end walls.

■ Paint stripes across the floor between the two narrow walls to increase the impression of width in the room.

Cool (receding) colours
Violet
Blue-violet
Blue
Blue-green
Green

Remember that large-scale patterns will dominate a small area. In a small room it is better to choose a small-scale design with a pale background that allows the eye to pass through the pattern. When a dining area forms part of the kitchen, decorating that corner in patterned wallpaper (in a complementary shade to the kitchen walls) helps to give it a more relaxed and cosy feel.

Choosing a pattern

When space is short there are a few more rules to remember when it comes to choosing patterns. These points are just as valid whether you are wallpapering or considering stamping or stencilling a design over painted walls.

■ Unless you want to make a bold statement, opt for small-scale prints on wallpaper. Large prints can be quite overpowering and will make the wall space appear smaller, as well as giving the walls an advancing effect.

■ Choose a pattern with a light coloured background to increase the sense of space.

■ Go for patterns that encourage the eye to look 'through' them, making the space appear larger – an open design on a light background is most effective at increasing the impression of space.

■ Satin-finish papers (or painted backgrounds) will reflect the light better than matt finishes, making the room appear lighter and larger.

Don't let all of these do's and don'ts discourage you from being bold with your choice of patterns. Mixing and matching patterns will create a more personal and creative scheme, and you cannot fail if you put together several from the same colourway, and keep to classic patterns such as spots and stripes, checks and florals. Just remember to keep the scale of the patterns small.

Staying neutral

If you are still feeling confused by colour, take heart, for there are other options open to you. While we have been focusing attention on the colour wheel and its various divisions, a smaller, yet very important, sector has been ignored – the neutrals. Black, white and shades of grey and cream are often passed over, yet they are important, not only for the part they can play in the type of colour schemes we have

Neutral colour schemes work well in open-plan apartments or dual-purpose rooms, because the neutral walls allow you to add different splashes of colour in the separate living areas. This neutral scheme creates a light, airy feel, but the natural wood stops it looking cold and uninteresting.

already mentioned but also in creating 'colour' schemes in their own right.

Neutrals are useful not only because they are so flexible but also because they can fit into most schemes, albeit in a small way, without jarring the eye or screaming for attention. Think how successfully a cast iron fireplace sits against any colour of wall or of the way fresh, white woodwork creates a smart, bright contrast with any choice of palette. If you are in a quandary about what colour to use for your finishing touches, turn to the neutrals and you won't go far wrong. Or, why not go one step further, and decorate a whole room with a neutral colour scheme? Whites, creams and shades of coffee can be combined to create an elegant and sophisticated look or a fresh and simple one, especially when the scheme is combined with natural wood furniture and a natural flooring, such as wood or tiles.

Textures

The key to creating an interesting scheme is not only to put together a variety of shades but also to incorporate a variety of textures. It's easy to become so wrapped up in your deliberations about what colours will suit a scheme that you forget another important consideration – texture. From wools and linens to satins, velvets and silks, there is such a range of different textured fabrics available that it is a positive sin to ignore them. Cover a sofa with satin scatter cushions and it may look attractive and colourful, but mix and match cushion covers made from cottons, velvets and needlepoint and it becomes much more exciting. Texture stimulates both our sense of sight and touch, adding an extra dimension to your design and giving it added depth. And, if you are working with a neutral or harmonious colour scheme, you need to introduce texture to bring the look to life.

Textures will change subtly as the light falling on them alters, creating an ever-changing mood. Shadows cast by pools of light will emphasize their textural qualities, while a direct light will flatten out subtle rises and falls – something else to bear in mind when you are planning your lighting scheme.

Do not forget, however, that fabrics are not the only source of texture – the hard surfaces you introduce into your room have their own textures that you can use to enhance your colour scheme. Like colour, textures can be divided into two categories, warm and cool. The cool textures generally appear to be the most luxurious. These are the shiny finishes, such as glass, chrome, glazed tiles and mirrored glass. Warm textures are non-reflective, such as wood, wool, tweed and brick.

A successful interior will have a good mixture of warm and cool textures, as well as complementary colours, so look at ways of mixing the rough with the smooth as well as the patterned with the plain.

Combine muslin, voile, cotton and lace with shiny chintz and smooth silk to furnish a bedroom (hanging lengths of muslin or lace behind your bedroom curtains, adds textural interest as well as providing you with more privacy). Or mix wool and linen with chenille and velvet to accessorize a living room. And look out for fabrics with textural details, or accessories with unusual edgings, trimmings and tie-backs. They will all work for you in creating a more interesting and successful scheme.

In a one-room apartment or a small room it can be hard to ring the changes. Cushions and throws can help you achieve a different look from season to season, and you do not have to spend a fortune or move all the furniture around. The warm textures of these accessories complement and enhance the wood.

3 Creating a style

A traditional home will often resist attempts to streamline rooms or introduce a sense of spaciousness. If your home has traditional features, make the most of them and continue the theme. You can create storage space in even the smallest nooks and crannies, and don't forget to use the ceiling too!

Now that you have planned what you need in order to make your new interior work practically, you can, finally, allow yourself to think about how you want your room to look. It may be that this is the stage you've been anxious to get on with and you simply can't wait to start putting your ideas into practice. On the other hand, the prospect of creating a 'look' for your home may be enough to send you scuttling for cover. Whatever your feelings, there are enough suggestions and tips on the following pages to make even the most nervous take heart and, if you follow the guidelines in this chapter, you will soon be creating stylish interiors with ease.

The key is to establish just two points: what style of interior appeals to you most and what colours you want to use. Once you have made those decisions, you can, if you wish, add one further element – a theme – although you may find that your ideas for a theme develop anyway while you are considering the first two points.

Choosing a style

In very general terms, you can classify the designs for most interiors as falling into one of the following groups:

■ Cottage or farmhouse: a rustic, charming look that uses small-scale patterns in natural fabrics and basic wooden furniture.

■ Country home: a grander country look with an air of shabby chic. The furniture may be antique, but it looks well used, and the soft furnishings have a faded elegance.

■ Town house: a bright, fresh and stylish look that draws on a mixture of contemporary and more traditional pieces.

■ Mediterranean: this cool and open scheme, with simple styling, uses bright, bold colours. The floors are bare and the furniture is simple. This sort of interior needs to be filled with warm sunlight to bring it to life.

■ International style: open plan and contemporary, homes in the International style are often decorated with expensive items in reflective materials, such as glass and chrome, and complemented by luxurious materials.

■ Retro: quirky and imaginative, the Retro look usually draws on a comparatively recent decade such as the 1950s or 1960s for its inspiration, and auction houses and junk shops are common sources for its furniture.

Within these broad categories there are, of course, many, many styles to choose from – you might, for example, favour the Arts & Crafts Movement or prefer Shaker-style simplicity. Your existing furniture might suggest that a Victorian theme would be appropriate for one room or you might be resolutely

Your choice of decor can emphasize the proportions of a small, traditional space or even re-create them. This modern bedroom has been decorated in a style that attempts to create the small cottage look. Taking a patterned wallpaper up and over the ceiling has the effect of lowering its perceived height.

curtaining shown in the photographs, but you can still take inspiration from the overall look and pick out the elements that appeal to you.

You may find it helpful to cut out the illustrations of styles and accessories that particularly appeal and keep them filed somewhere – perhaps in the folders you are keeping for each room's redesign, together with the room plan and measurements. As time goes by you may notice the same styles and themes appearing time and time again in your folder or scrapbook, and you may find that your preferred style does fall into one of the classifications suggested above. Even if you cannot actually define the look you want, you will at least have a better idea of the kind of look that you want to achieve.

Architectural inspiration

You may, of course, find yourself hankering after the Gothic mansions or looking longingly at the pretty farmhouses you find illustrated in the books and magazines you pick up and so becoming more and more disheartened with your postwar accommodation. Be positive! At least you have decided that you love the country cottage or the Victorian Gothic look, and there is no reason why you shouldn't adapt those preferences for your own design in some way. The framework of your living space need not necessarily dictate to you how you decorate it. As we saw in Chapter 2, the clever use of colour can perform convincing optical illusions, and you are free to use any of these to create the scale and mood of room you dream of.

Just one word of caution at this stage, however: you should, if at all possible, live in your home for a while before you make any major decorating decisions. The longer you are there, the more of a feel you will get for it and the styles that would suit it. In a small space especially, certain styles will be

Modern and want to change the look with every passing season.

If you don't immediately find yourself deciding on one style or another, it may help if you spend some time looking around you more critically and make notes of what appeals to you. Begin by looking through home-interest books and magazines for inspiration. When you see a room setting that appeals to you, analyse it more carefully and ask yourself why you like it. Is it the combination of colours, the window dressing or the way the furniture has been arranged? You may not be able to buy the actual furniture or inappropriate unless you are very careful to choose furniture and colours that are in keeping not only with the look but with the scale of your living space.

You may be fortunate enough to live in a property that dates from an era that provides enough inspiration in itself for your scheme. The 1970s saw a rush for open-plan living and flat, plain walls, but there is currently more sympathy for traditional features and many are being restored. So, if your tiny home boasts cast iron fireplaces, wooden panelled doors and deep skirting boards, you have the blueprint for your scheme already in place. You can go against the grain by all means, but if you are still unsure what direction to take, why not follow the obvious route, and allow yourself to be inspired by the period, and recreate the Victorian cottage or town house – there are plenty of source books, not to mention films and TV dramas from which you can gather inspiration for the details.

The advantage of using the historical references provided by your home as your starting point is that they will never date – and you can always add more up-to-the-minute touches in the furnishings or colours you use to keep the look exciting.

Re-creating history

If you like the idea of re-creating the feel of a certain period in your home, why not take it one step further and focus on a particular fashion or movement within that era. Throughout history there have always been groups of people who have reacted against the mainstream beliefs and designs of their time to produce something that, at the time especially, was quite startlingly and refreshingly different. Think of the Bauhaus, the Shakers and the Arts & Crafts movement. Many of these designs look just as good today as when they were first developed, and they are ripe for replicating in your own

home. Perhaps you already have a Shaker-style kitchen or a simple wooden chest of drawers that is reminiscent of the look – it could inspire you to continue the style throughout one room or even your whole living space. Perhaps you have always loved the Liberty prints, which were originally designed by William Morris, in which case some research into the Arts & Crafts movement may encourage you to develop the theme further.

Browse through historical design books to learn more about the styles of the past, and you may discover just the inspiration you are looking for.

If the proportions of your home are on the small side, you need to think carefully before taking on the look of another era in its entirety. It is worth maintaining and highlighting existing traditional features, but the deeper, more sombre shades favoured by the Victorians are not always the best choice for a small, gloomy hallway.

A small room will appear larger if it is furnished with low-level sofas, which allow the eye to pass over and beyond them to the extremities of the room. Even a small room needs to be given some height, however, to make it interesting and to provide balance. Here a picture draws the eye upwards, while the coordinating cushions create a unified look.

Waiting to be discovered

Just as the basic framework of your home is often just waiting to be recognized as a source of inspiration, it may be that your existing furniture is just the starting point you need. Try to look at the pieces within your room with a fresh eye – especially those that you have decided you want to include in your new scheme or cannot afford to replace. Look at your furniture in the light of any research you may have already done into the various looks for interiors. Do you possess anything that suggests a certain style of furnishing? If so, can you capitalize on it?

A limited budget can often work in your favour, because it will force you to seek inspiration from, and to be more creative with, what you have already got. Could your floral curtains be the starting point for a country house interior? Does your heavy wooden bed frame suggest a traditional Tudor look? Try to view your furniture and furnishings in an impartial way, rather than looking at them from a sentimental viewpoint. This will allow you to see beyond their face value, and it may also help to see that an item could work better for you if it were adapted in some way. A chest, for example, could be repainted or a chair could be reupholstered to make your new look more successful.

What colours to use

If you have read the previous chapter on colour, you should already be feeling more confident about your ability to put together a colour scheme. But if you are not, don't worry – creating a successful colour scheme can just be a matter of copying. No, it's not cheating; it is more a matter of getting into the habit of looking and learning from what is all around you. Remember, nothing is original. What initially may appear to be a very daring colour scheme of pink and deep green suddenly seems less original when you spot a bunch of pretty pink rosebuds nearby, their heads pressed up against the vivid green leaves.

Your first experiments with bold shades can be quite nerve racking, but if you take a look around, you will soon begin to notice how even the most daring combinations can be successful. The colours of nature are always a good starting point – so look at the colours in a bowl of fruit or a vase of flowers and see which combinations appeal to you.

A small attic bedroom is brought to life by a profusion of red roses. If you want a fancy bed dressing, don't let the small proportions of your bedroom deter you. A simple dressing hung from a pole above the bed adds height and interest without dominating the room.

Nature knows

Looking at nature for inspiration is a very good way to start researching your colour scheme, because nature never gets it wrong. If autumn is your favourite season, the palette for your home should consist of bright oranges, yellow ochres, berry reds and golden-browns, perhaps with a dash of sky blue or emerald green. If you are more of a spring person, look for daffodil or primrose yellows and team them with iris blue or tulip red. Anyone who likes the warmth and cosiness of winter need look no further than a sprig of holly in order to feel happy with their choice of deep red and green. If you have four rooms, you could even decorate each one to represent one of the four seasons. As long as you remember the effects of warm and cool colours in your home and take into account the way a room faces, you won't go wrong.

Other sources

If the garden isn't offering you much in the way of inspiration, turn to your existing furnishings. You may wish that you could afford some new curtains, but it is possible that the ones that are already up are just the starting point you need. If they are made of patterned fabric, the colour scheming is already done for you. Take the main colour as the basis of your theme, and use one or two other colours within the design as accent colours on your skirting boards, dado rail, cushions and lampshades.

If the curtains are plain, you have a bit more freedom. Turn back to the colour wheel on page 27 and look at what colours would work with the shade of your curtain fabric. If you would like a sophisticated, harmonious colour scheme, pick different shades of the same colour with which to make up the rest of the soft furnishings or a colour that lies next to the base colour on the colour wheel. If you want something more vibrant, look to the opposite side of the colour wheel from your fabric colour and use whatever lies there as your accent colour. The window dressings can easily dominate a small room, and to avoid this use a related shade on the walls next to

your curtains and keep the accent colour for the furniture and smaller furnishings.

Do not restrict your search for inspiration to existing fabrics. Look at pictures, china and even a bowl of fruit to find colour combinations that appeal to you. A few bananas sitting in a blue glass bowl may be the only clue needed to set you on course for a successful yellow and blue scheme. It's easy when you know how!

Adding a theme

Some rooms in particular will benefit from having a theme imposed on them, and this can be the basis of the style of your room and the colours you use in it, adding interest and cohesion to your design. Rooms where you want to relax usually require slightly more subtle styling than a quirky theme provides, but busy, lively rooms, such as children's bedrooms, kitchens and bathrooms, are very well suited to being given a very distinctive look. Look carefully at these rooms in particular for a possible starting point before you make any other decorating decisions.

Bathrooms may cry out for a nautical or water-related theme, which you can capitalize on with suitable accessories, such as fish-shaped soap dishes, heavy ship's rope suspended along the walls and collections of sea shells dotted around the room. If you are really brave, you could even go for an appropriately designed painted mural, to give bathers something fun to focus on.

In the kitchen you might take your cue from something more food related, such as fruit, vegetables or even wine. Appropriate stencils, stamps, tiles or wallpaper borders are a good way of continuing a theme on your wall space, and in a small kitchen-dining room an intimate bistro theme could be continued into the dining area with bistro-style posters on the walls.

It may be that you already have a collection to display or one cherished item that you

---

Sources of inspiration

☐ Home-interest magazines

☐ The age and architectural style of your home

☐ Other styles of architecture

☐ Historical trends

☐ The style of your existing furniture and furnishings

☐ The colours of nature

☐ The colours in your existing furnishings, a picture or a favourite piece of china

A collection of wooden treasures has brought the dining side of this open-plan room to life. Make the most of your open-plan or dual-purpose spaces by giving a different theme or focus to small areas within the room and use them to create 'room' dividers. These two areas are clearly defined, not only by the half-height wall and different approach to decor, but also by the change in the flooring and lighting.

can exploit. A straw doll may inspire a Folk Art look, complete with gingham tea towels and checked table linen, while a blue and white Wedgwood plate might encourage you to create a more sophisticated, classical look. Sometimes a colour combination alone may be all the theme you need.

Your children won't need much encouragement to come up with ideas for their own rooms. Try if you can to restrict their fantasies so that a room is not decorated to reflect a passing phase. If possible, encourage them to turn to themes that have stood the test of

time, such as the Wild West or a fantasy castle, rather than cartoon characters that may fall from favour as quickly as they rose from obscurity. Make your own stencils or potato print stamps to decorate the walls if you cannot find what you want in the shops, and let the children help you if they are old enough.

The advantage of having a theme is that it takes some of the decision making out of your hands. Once you have established the look, the types of furnishings and fittings you choose to complete it have to follow suit in order to achieve a successful, balanced look.

Shelving need not be bulky or obtrusive, and it can be efficient and look attractive too. Use slim-line, small-scale shelving and smart hooks to make the most of limited wall space.

Let your room develop

In many homes, the room that looks the most welcoming and attractive is the one that has been allowed to develop over a period of time – or at least gives that impression. A well-designed interior looks lived in and loved – quite the opposite of many show houses or hotel rooms, which, although designed by a professional, are essentially soulless. By decorating your own living space for yourself, you have one important advantage over the professional interior designer – you have time on your side. In addition, because you actually live in the space that is being decorated, you can gather inspiration over a matter of months and add extra touches as time goes by.

Accessories are very important to all homes, no matter how small. The trick is being able to differentiate between accessories and clutter! A small room will not work if it is overcrowded with bits and pieces that do little to enhance its effect, but any size of room will benefit from the addition of a few carefully chosen ornaments or artefacts that reflect and complement the decoration around the room – and add a little of your own personality too.

4 The bedroom

Creating a raised platform area is an excellent way of creating two rooms out of one if your ceilings are high enough to accommodate the extra level. It also offers the opportunity to create storage space within the platform, possibly even for a bed. In dual-function spaces it is important to make each 'room' work efficiently or neither will be successful. Remember details such as having adequate lighting for reading during the day and a bedside light at night.

No matter what size it is, the bedroom should be the room in which you feel most at home. A room where you can relax and dream, it is your personal haven. Unfortunately, however, the demands of modern living have meant that bedroom space is increasingly viewed as something of a luxury and, as a result, it has not only become more restricted but is also frequently used as a dual-purpose space, being combined with either a workstation or a living area. Even when it is used as nothing more than a place to sleep, dress and store clothes, the available bedroom space is put under a certain amount of pressure, but once it is shared by two people and utilized in some secondary way, it becomes a real challenge to the designer.

Effective planning

To get the most out of your bedroom, the first task is to establish exactly what your needs and wishes are – and don't forget to incorporate a bit of luxury. Turn to Chapter 1 again, and look at the questions you should be asking about the way the sleeping area in your home is used. Look at your list, and make sure that you have thought about the following requirements:

■ Space to sleep.

■ Storage space for clothes (and possibly suitcases, hatboxes, out-of-season clothes and the like).

■ Dressing space, including room in front of a mirror.

■ Making up or shaving space (unless you prefer to do this in the bathroom).

■ Seating (ranging from a simple chair to a sofa, depending on your needs).

■ A dressing-table (perhaps doubling as a desk).

■ Room for a small television.

You may also want to consider the use of the bedroom space in terms of what the rest of your accommodation offers. For example, if bathroom space in your home is in short supply or great demand, would a corner of your bedroom be best utilized by the addition of a hand basin or even a shower area?

Once you have finalized your list, you can start planning how to best design your space, incorporating everything in it, plus follow-on requirements such as telephone points and electric sockets for lighting and gadgets such as hair-dryers, shavers, televisions and so on.

Be as imaginative and practical as possible in your planning, although, realistically, small bedrooms do not offer much scope for flexibility, largely because the few pieces you are juggling with – bed, wardrobe and so on – are so large and bulky.

It is usual to avoid putting the head of a bed directly under a window or up against a radiator (to avoid both draughts and over-heating), but this may immediately eliminate two of the four walls, and if one of the other two walls has either a fireplace or an awkwardly placed door in it, you are likely to be left with just one option. You may need to consider moving a badly placed radiator if it is restricting you at every turn, or, if you don't like a warm bedroom, you could put a piece of furniture permanently in front of it. Look at the position of your doorway, too. Would moving it slightly open up a lot more possibilities? By thinking three-dimensionally you may discover you have a lot more space to play with than you originally imagined.

If you have a single bed, you will have more freedom of choice, as the bed has to be accessed from only one side and so can be put alongside a wall, thus opening up the rest of the room. Remember, however, that with any size of bed, you are likely to want a bedside-table on at least one side, so allow space for this.

In a small bedroom you can make the most of the available space if you are aware of the minimum width needed to pass between pieces of furniture comfortably. The recommended minimum circulation space around a bed is 56cm (22in), while the required standing space in front of a hand basin is 61cm (24in). Try to avoid having everything so tight that getting from one side of the room to the other is like getting around an obstacle course, or the bedroom will become somewhere you can't wait to get out of, rather than somewhere you go to relax. If you have already

A design such as this would suit either a small bedroom or a bedsitting room. It will cost a little more to have a custom-made bed designed and made, but it not only creates a focal point but also provides plenty of storage and display solutions.

bought your furniture or have measured it up in the shop, use your scaled plans (see Chapter 1) to check that there is room to open wardrobe doors easily and to sit comfortably at a dressing-table. Beds are usually a standard length, 1.9m (6ft 3in), and in a choice of 0.9m (3ft), 1.4m (4ft 6in) and 1.5m (5ft) widths. If you don't yet know how big your furniture will be, leaf through a few catalogues. You will soon get an idea of the average size of a double or single wardrobe to use as a rough guide.

The right style of bed

Choosing a bed for a small bedroom can be quite a challenge because beds inevitably take up so much space. Before you start looking at the various styles of bed, take another look at the space that is available and consider if you could utilize it more effectively by being more imaginative. Is there room to incorporate a raised sleeping platform so that you can use all your floor space for other furniture and activities? Platform beds can create extra space below for hanging clothes, for incorporating a desk or seating area or for providing extra storage space. They are ideal for bedsitting rooms because the sleeping area is kept distinct from the rest of the room. If you are unsure about installing a permanent platform, take a look at bunk-style beds, which are ready-made into a bed and desk combination. If you contact a bed manufacturer or carpenter direct you may find that you can have beds and units such as this made to your own specifications, so that a bedroom that is only 1.8m (6ft) wide is not an insuperable problem.

In order to create an impression of space it is better if the eye can travel freely over the room and the furniture in it, and this makes heavy four-poster beds and chunky sleigh beds less preferable than more delicately framed and lower styles of bed. Futons and other low oriental styles are ideal for small bedrooms, but if you cannot resist a four-poster and have the space to incorporate it, look at contemporary cast iron designs and leave the frame bare or minimally draped

with sheer fabrics, rather than blocking the line of vision with heavy bed curtains. Even tall head- and foot-boards, such as those on a traditional Victorian bedstead, should be avoided unless you are happy for the bed to dominate the room.

If you are choosing a single bed, consider a style that allows you to present it as a sofa, piled with cushions during the day, an approach that is especially appropriate if you are designing a bedsit area. The simplest

Attic bedrooms often have high pitched ceilings, and emphasizing this height with a traditional bedstead will takes the eye upwards and add a certain grandeur. This arrangement makes the best possible use of every inch of available space. Small pictures suit the limited wall space, while bedside tables provide room for lamps and knick-knacks.

styles that have no head- or foot-board are most adaptable, but some day beds offer sleeping facilities combined with an elegant sofa design. If you often have overnight visitors, take a look at designs that conceal a replica single bed beneath the frame.

Choosing for comfort

You will spend an unbelievable one-third of your lifetime in bed, so make sure that you consider comfort as much as style when you choose your bed. Experiment with different bases and different mattresses until you find a combination that feels right. Putting one type of mattress on a different base and vice versa can make a significant difference to the feel of the bed.

Types of mattress

There are two basic types of mattress – those with a sprung interior and those made of only foam, fibre or latex. Regular-use mattresses should have a sprung interior and these are also divided into two types, pocket springs and open springs:

■ Pocket springs: the springs in these mattresses are housed in little fabric pockets that move independently so that your body is sup-ported where it needs it, and your partner does not move every time you do. They are generally more expensive than open-spring mattresses.

■ Open springs: these mattresses are the most often seen. The firmness varies tremendously according to the numbers of springs used and the gauge of the wire.

Styles of base

■ Slatted: these offer good ventilation for the mattress, which makes them good for anyone suffering from an allergy, but they need to be combined with a mattress that is specially designed for a slatted base.

■ Firm edge: a wood- or metal-framed base with springs placed within it is known as a firm-edge base. Traditional iron bedsteads would have had a sprung base within a firm edge.

■ Sprung edge: this is the luxurious option. The springs come right up to the edge of the mattress, widening the sleeping area and increasing the degree of support offered.

Storage for small bedrooms

Clothes and shoes create the greatest storage problems in the bedroom, and few rooms offer enough permanent hanging space to cope with two people's wardrobes. If you have a loft or underbed storage space, it is worth investing in some good quality clothes storage bags and acid-free tissue paper and keeping out-of-season clothes hidden from sight. Some companies produce specially designed underbed storage units, which can be wheeled in and out on castors.

Free-standing wardrobes are generally inadequate if you have a large collection of clothes – especially bulky suits – as they seldom offer enough hanging space for even one, let alone two people. Look at the layout of your room and assess what it offers in the way of storage potential to supplement or

The alcoves at the sides of a chimney breast are always useful for adding wardrobe space, and painting them the same colour as the walls helps to create an integrated look. If you prefer a softer effect, choose a curtain rather than a solid wood front.

replace your existing wardrobes. Alcoves, especially those on either side of a chimney breast, are the obvious places to exploit, and they can easily be converted into permanent wardrobes with a solid wooden door or, more easily, fitted with a hanging rail and a curtain front. Look too at the space you have at the bottom of your existing hanging space. Is there room to incorporate a two-tier hanging system where there once was only one rail? Or could you add a set of drawers or shelves to create extra space for folded items?

If you are to make the most of your available space, the best option may well be to have fitted wardrobes installed. Although the term 'fitted wardrobe' is unfortunately reminiscent of the worst of 1970s design, you do not *have* to opt for melamine or louvered door fronts. Today there is such a choice of good materials and finishes that you are sure to find one that fits your sense of style while offering you more storage space than you imagined possible. In

fact, if they are well planned and designed, a range of wall units can add interest to an otherwise characterless room structure.

The main advantage of the streamlined fitted unit is that it can conceal anything, from suitcases and hat boxes to shoes and hair-dryers – with the most sophisticated designs even housing dressing-tables, work-stations and television sets. Clutter makes a room seem even smaller than it actually is, so a bit of streamlining could transform the look of your room – and even your lifestyle, as it is so much easier to be organized when there is a space for everything.

Another advantage to having custom-designed storage space is that it will help you overcome problems such as tight corners and awkward angles through the use of bi-folding doors, carousel units and other clever details. Ask several companies to quote for the work you want carried out and see which comes up with the most imaginative ideas.

Floor finishes

A bedroom is the one place you can afford to be a bit more indulgent with your flooring – and you should be. After all, you have only a small area to cover if your bedroom is not very large. The worst wear and tear most bedrooms have to cope with is some barefooted padding around in the morning and evening and perhaps the occasional spilled make-up or breakfast tea, so you should be able to spend your money on something fairly luxurious, if that suits the look you are planning.

Carpeting is the favourite floor covering for most bedrooms, offering softness and warmth underfoot and a sense of wall-to-wall comfort. In small rooms look for plain or very small patterned carpeting in cool colours to increase the impression of space in the room and do buy the best you can afford. It may be worth investing in some cheap, soft rugs to place in areas that get most wear or are most likely to attract spills, such as at the side of the bed and around a dressing table and wardrobe.

As you are carpeting only a small area, do not skimp on the underlay you choose. Underlay increases a carpet's life, makes it softer underfoot and improves its insulating qualities. Foam-backed carpets are a far inferior choice and have a much shorter life-span.

Well-designed fitted units create a streamlined look in a small space and are ideal for concealing all kinds of clutter. They are also ideal for one-room living because the door fronts can hide anything from a kitchen centre to a tiny bathroom when those areas are not in use, allowing you greater flexibility with the decoration of the open space.

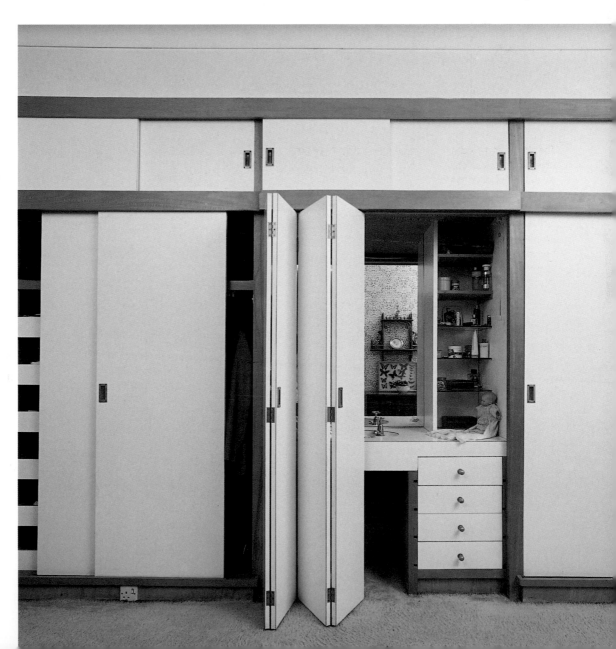

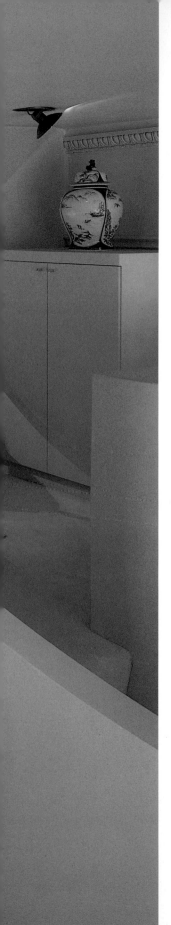

Mirrored glass is useful when you are working with a limited space, and it can be used, as here, to reflect light back into the bedroom space. Good bedroom lighting should emphasize the best points of a room, such as any decorative features, as well as being practical.

Hard flooring, such as wood strip, boards or parquet, is ideal for a traditional-looking bedroom, whether your preference is for the Shaker style or a simple Victorian look, and it almost always increases the impression of space in a room. However, for comfort underfoot on a chilly morning, hard flooring is not the best choice for a bedroom, unless it is combined with rugs, which can create a more bitty and less spacious effect.

Lighting effects

Well-planned lighting is essential in the bedroom. Not only can carefully positioned lighting help create the right atmosphere but it can provide the right level of illumination for practical tasks such as making up, reading and mixing and matching clothes. One central pendent light may seem adequate for a small bedroom, but it will tend to produce a flat, dull and harsh effect, wasting all the effort you have put into choosing the right fabrics, wallpaper and accessories.

Take another look at your notes to remind yourself what you want the lighting to achieve. Essentially, it needs to be flexible so that, at the flick of a switch, the room can be transformed from a practical workplace or dressing room, into a cosy or romantic haven – and ideally it shouldn't take up valuable floor or storage space. Wall lights that can be controlled by a dimmer switch are the perfect solution – especially at the bedside – as they eliminate the need for bedside-table space and can create a range of moods. If you like to read in bed, look for shades that direct the light mostly downwards, and if your partner likes to sleep while you read, make sure that the lights are separately controlled at the bedside. Adjustable spot-lights are a less attractive option for the bedroom, but they have the advantage of being multi-angled so you can direct the glare onto a page without disturbing anyone else.

Remember that the way the floorboards run emphasizes either the width or the breadth of the room. In some rooms this could work in your favour, but in others it may draw attention to the room's narrowness rather than its spaciousness. Although bare boards are practical and suit a traditional-style room, if they run the wrong way, you may be better investing in a piece of plain carpet.

If the size of your window is not suited to a grand scale of dressing, there is no reason why you cannot go to town on the bed-head instead. This treatment emphasizes the height of the room without encroaching on the space around the bed. Small recessed windows, such as this can be left plain or given special treatment (see page 62).

When you are applying make-up, the lighting should ideally be directed onto you and your face, so position your wall lights to either side of the mirror for best results. For dressing, however, it is important that the light illuminates you and not the mirror, so consider fitting a ceiling light – a recessed spot-light is an unobtrusive solution – at a point between the mirror and where you normally stand.

If your bedroom is also a study or workroom, consider what sort of lighting best suits your practical needs. Adjustable lighting, such as free-standing spot-lights, offer the greatest flexibility for working at a desk. A desk lamp may be the best option, or you could consider floor-standing lighting (with either a pendent shade to cast light downwards or a collection of mini spot-lights), which could be moved around the room to be used elsewhere, perhaps behind an armchair or sofa, at other times of the day. Whenever possible, avoid using your work light source as part of your permanent lighting scheme, because when you want to relax, the last thing you need to see illuminated is a computer or a pile of papers.

Window dressings

The bedroom offers wonderful opportunities to be as bold as you dare with your choice of window dressing. Unless you are decorating a spare bedroom, you can look on this space as your personal retreat and somewhere you can indulge your fancies. Remember, too, that you are more likely to see the curtains closed in this room than any other, so their effect when drawn together is important.

Practically speaking, the curtains in your

bedroom should provide privacy, warmth and, perhaps, darkness. If your bedroom is overlooked, think about combining fabric drapes with translucent blinds, lace panels or swathes of muslin for extra privacy. If warmth is an issue, consider thermal linings and heavier fabrics to keep out the draughts. If you like to lie in until noon, the black-out qualities of whatever you choose will be important; but if you prefer to wake up bathed in sunlight, heavy curtains will be less of a priority.

The small bedroom can impose other practical restrictions on your design. The size of the window or the small scale of the room is likely to rule out grand, extravagant styles, such as swags and tails, and require that your creativity is directed more towards imaginative headings, shaped pelmets or pretty Roman or festoon blinds. Your choice of pole finial and tie-backs also offer opportunities to add more frivolous touches. If you cannot resist a touch of grandeur, you could always add a simple swag of muslin over your curtain headings, or gather a length of fabric and drape it through two swag holders, creating a bunched rosette effect where it comes through the holders. If the window is very small or the room is very dark, you could combine a fancy swag with a simple roller or Roman blind and forget about curtains entirely.

If you work or entertain in your bedroom during the day, the amount of natural light that the room receives will be more important than it would be in a single-function room, so full curtains and impressive pelmets that shade much of the window area may make the room too dark. Instead, opt for simpler designs and use tie-backs to let the light flood in. You could extend your pole or track beyond the window frame so that the curtains do not obscure the glass at all, or, if warmth is not an issue, consider fitting a set of folding shutters. Louvered, folding designs

will give you greater control over the amount of light and privacy the room receives while taking up minimal space.

Many small bedrooms have been created in the roof space and so produce their own particular set of window dressing problems in the form of skylights. Privacy is unlikely to be a problem, but insulation and light control will be important aspects to consider. Curtains are seldom a viable proposition because it is almost always impossible to open and close them satisfactorily unless the window is within easy reach, so an attractive blind is your best option. Some skylight manufacturers produce their own ready-made roller blinds to fit into the recess, and these can be personalized by making your own window surround-cum-pelmet from a material such as 6mm (¼in) medium density fibreboard (MDF), which can be painted or covered in fabric.

There is no need to sacrifice a sense of grandeur simply because your space is limited. Look out for pieces that suggest a grand scheme but that have been created on a smaller scale. The mirror, with its traditional mouldings, adds depth to a study/bedroom, and the small cottage window has been given a dramatic touch with floor-length curtains, wisely made from pale fabric so they do not overpower the room.

This open-plan living space has been created with the structural support pillars still in place. Although this was no doubt a necessary compromise, the pillars help to create separate pockets of living space within the one room. You could consider adding mock structural supports, decorative columns or half walls to separate sleeping and working areas.

Tiny recessed windows that are within reach, such as are often found in attic bedrooms and small, old cottages, need to be left as uncluttered by fabric as possible so that light can still filter into the room. Such windows can, however, be curtained in one of two ways if you want. First, if there is enough room at both sides of the window, curtains can be hung on a pole set outside the recess. Alternatively, if the depth of the recess is more than half the width of the window, you can hang curtains on swing arms that open up flat against the walls of the recess when they are opened. You could even fit the swing arms with two fabrics – one to be seen when the arms are open during the day and the other to be seen at night.

Some small windows can even be made to appear something that they are not with the right sort of dressing. If your window is rather lacking in height, for example, check how much wall space you have between the top of it and the ceiling. If you have an adequate space, you could add a dressy pelmet above the window frame, positioning it so that it does not obscure any of the glass, and this will give instant height and grandeur to the window.

Bedsitting rooms

The first question to ask yourself when you are redesigning a bedsitting room is whether you want a bedroom where you also want to live, or a living room where you also want to sleep? It is most likely that you will want the latter, and if this is the case you should also look at Chapter 5 on living rooms.

As with all dual-purpose rooms, the key to successful design lies in making a clear distinction between the two areas and functions, so that neither appears to be a compromise when it is being used. In other words, once you go to bed in your bedsitting room it should offer you as much comfort and feel as much like a bedroom as any single-function bedroom should do. Equally, during the day, the bed or bedroom area should ideally be invisible or at least clearly separated from the working space.

If the room is large enough and allows it, consider how you might define the two areas visually with your choice of decoration, furnishings or floor coverings. Could the sleeping area be decorated in softer, more romantic tones of the main living room colour or by the use of a different print? Perhaps the floor in the bedroom area could be distinguished by the addition of some soft rugs? If the living area has a hard floor, you might want to consider carpeting the sleeping area.

A quick and easy way of separating a permanent sleeping area is by the use of a folding screen or, if the room is large enough, you could even add a partition wall, complete with folding doors or glass doors. Glass bricks are becoming a popular – although rather expensive – way of incorporating a partition without sacrificing light, or you could have a partition wall built from panes of glass, fitted in an attractive frame. An alternative and less permanent solution is to experiment with the positioning of your furniture to create a visual barrier between the two areas. It will make the room far more interesting if the whole area cannot be taken in at once.

Sleeping comfortably

If the main function of your room is to provide living and seating space, you will want a bed that can be easily concealed during the

Sofa beds are a good buy for a bedsitting room or a room that has to function as both a guest room and, perhaps, a study. If it is going to be used on a regular basis, buy the best you can afford – you generally get what you pay for.

In a dual-purpose room, a bed can be dressed so that it looks like a sofa during the day. Cover the bed with a throw and pile the length of it with cushions for a back rest. Bolsters are particularly useful because they can mimic sofa armrests. Consider making a more permanent back-rest from a piece of thick foam, cut to size and covered with fabric. It can be fixed to a piece of hardboard or medium density fibreboard for stability.

day and ideally one that can be cleared away in order to leave as much room as possible for daily activities. Choose a bed that is as unobtrusive as possible, and covering it with bed linen or a throw-over that blends well with the wall colour or decoration will help you achieve this. Platform sleeping areas and bunk bed arrangements have already been discussed as good ways of incorporating a sleeping space that is not only out of view but that offers extra usable floor space. Other possibilities include the wall-stored, fold-away bed and the sofa bed. Today, wall-stored beds smack somewhat of James Bond films and 1970s storage solutions, but they are worth considering if you are anxious to have a very streamlined finish to the room.

A sofa bed (or a fold-out futon) is likely to be a more practical option for most people, but although there may be plenty on the market, spend some time carefully researching the styles that are within your budget. In a bedsitting room it is important that the piece you choose is just as comfortable as a bed at night as it is as a sofa during the day. Look for a design with a proper sprung mattress and a sturdy frame so that it will stand up to constant use. It is worth spending as much as you can afford. With both fold-away options, remember that you will have to spend precious time each day assembling and folding away the bed and that you need to have somewhere to store your bed linen.

Sitting pretty

If you prefer the idea of a permanent 'proper' bed and your living space is limited, your seating plan will have to be more flexible. Fold-away chairs are always useful, but they lack the comfort of a solid armchair or sofa. Large, upholstered footstools are a practical addition, as they can be used as a coffee table, as extra seating and, yes, even as a footstool now and then! Using a single bed against a wall, piled high with cushions as a back rest, is, as we have

seen, one way of providing more comfort for you and visitors, while large floor cushions and beanbags are useful extra seating when you need it. If you have frequent overnight visitors, two single beds placed at right angles to each other in the corner of a room and backed with scatter cushions will act as extra seating during the day as well as more sleeping space, or you may prefer to have a fold-away camp bed stored under a bed for occasional use.

A change of scene

Whatever your furniture or sleeping preferences, keep flexibility and adaptability your priorities when you shop. Bedsitting rooms can become tiresome because they do not offer the distraction of moving out of one room and into another, and you can soon tire of the decorations. If the furniture you choose is on castors or can easily be moved, and if it looks as attractive from the back as from the front and can be quickly given a new look with a fresh set of covers, it will offer welcome opportunities for the occasional change around.

Lighting the bedsitting room

It is vitally important to create practical and effective lighting schemes in dual-purpose rooms so that you are able to 'shut off' one part of the room and bring another into play with just the flick of a switch. In the bedsitting room especially, remember there will be times when you will want the sleeping area bathed in a soft romantic glow and certainly not given the same practical glare of lighting that the living area may require.

Think about creating soft pools of light in the sleeping area with candles, wall lights and table lamps fitted with low-wattage bulbs, and make sure that all the bedroom lighting is controlled from the bedside so that you do not have to cross the visual and mental barrier into the 'living room' to turn off the lights. Look at Chapter 5 on living rooms for suggestions on lighting that area.

5 The living room

Window seats are always worth considering when space is limited, especially if they offer extra storage space below. The look depends on the choice of fabric. The effect here is bright and casual, but a more sophisticated fabric and the matching bolsters would create a quite different impression.

Believe it or not, small living rooms *do* have advantages over larger ones. Most importantly, they offer the opportunity to create an intimate, warm and cosy room for both entertaining and relaxing in – and, of course, everyone can see the television, wherever they sit! The way you approach the design of your particular living room will depend very much on what you regularly demand from it, so before you start planning colour schemes, turn back to Chapter 1 on preparation and planning and use it to help you assess your basic requirements.

Listing your priorities for the living room is probably more difficult than it will be for any other room, not only because it is likely to be the room that your family uses the most, but because it is also the place that is most 'on show' to visitors. To help you on your way, the most common basic requirements are likely to be:

■ Seating for the family (and perhaps guests).

■ Reading areas.

■ Space for TV and hi-fi.

■ Space for entertaining guests.

■ Storage for books and other collections, including toys.

■ A desk or table for studying or serving snacks or dinner.

Now you need to work out how to incorporate these elements most successfully into your plan, remembering to include vital points such as sockets, radiators, TV aerials, telephone points and so on. Try to look at your room in a three-dimensional way so that you can fully assess its potential. Would moving a door release space for a storage unit or a desk? Could walls be added, removed or replaced by folding doors to make the living space more useful? Perhaps opening the living room up into your hallway would suit your needs better. Are the ceilings high? If so, is there room to incorporate a raised area that could be used for studying, dining or watching television and that is separated visually from the rest of the room?

These days lack of space forces us to use just one room for a multitude of activities that once might have been enjoyed in a series of separate rooms, so it has become even more of a challenge to create a living room design that works in both aesthetic and practical terms.

The seating plan

An important point to consider is your seating plan. Not only will your sofas and armchairs be the most bulky items you will have to position, but everything else, such as the siting of lighting points and the extra sockets and the TV points, will follow from there.

Take your room plan and scaled-down furniture templates (see Chapter 1) and play around with them until you find a good balance.

It will help if you can make your seating plan and the furniture you choose as flexible as possible so that you can cope with larger numbers when you are entertaining but can move pieces out of the way or fold them up when they are not in use, so that they do not fill up your limited space. Consider floor cushions and beanbags for extra seating, especially if you have children, and look for recesses, such as into a bay window, that would be suitable for a built-in seat, which could be designed to have a lift-up seat to provide extra storage space.

Good chairs for small rooms

□ Look out for chairs with small backs and gaps under the arms, rather than solid, bulky armchairs. Delicate designs allow the eye to pass through them to the room beyond. Rocking chairs, for example, may take up a lot of space, but the slats make them appear less bulky.

□ Folding chairs can be brought out whenever extra seating is required and kept out of sight when it is not.

□ Upholstered footstools can be used for extra seating and as somewhere to place books and magazines.

□ Designs with reclining backs offer space to sprawl when you want, but can be made more compact when necessary.

□ If you like the idea of flexible seating plans, castors make it easier to move chairs in and out from the edges of the room.

If you are yet to choose your furniture, you will have greater flexibility in working out your seating plan. If conversation and entertaining are priorities, do you have room for two small sofas or one sofa and two armchairs to face each other? This arrangement always creates a balanced and intimate design. Even more successful, however, is to have two small sofas placed at an angle to each other to form an L-shape. In a small room this is a sociable arrangement, allowing the focus of the sitters to be comfortably directed at each other, at a fireplace or at a television, and it also usually opens up a space for another chair to be added at the fourth corner, making it the most efficient and economical way of using the available area.

In a small living room, several small and different, or at least differently upholstered, pieces of furniture are a safer choice than the more conventional (and rather boring) three-piece suite, which can easily dominate a small room. Avoid especially trying to squeeze in a three-seater sofa. Instead, look at the possibility of combining a small sofa with two different styles of chair, such as a library-style armchair and a rocking chair or a Queen Anne-style chair with something more cosy.

Do not let your layout be restricted by convention and do not assume that all pieces of furniture should be pushed back against the walls of the room to create a free space in the centre. Your space may be limited, but you can still break a few rules. A sofa does not need to sit right back in a bay window if it would be more interesting to bring it forwards and put a small table behind it.

Other points to consider are the natural light the room receives, especially if you use the room frequently in daylight hours for studying or reading. There is little point in putting a favourite reading chair in the darkest corner of the room, unless you are happy to turn on artificial light every time you use

Even in this small room a pretty armchair has been accommodated next to a comfortable sofa, allowing shared use of the light cast from one table lamp. Hanging pictures and having shelves right up to ceiling level increases the perceived height of the room while creating a homely look. Even if your wall space is limited, pictures still look better when they are displayed in groups.

Small rooms require small-scale furniture or designs that allow the eye to pass through them, such as this slat-back chair. A cluttered room looks homely, but is not always easy to live with. As a rule, it is best to restrict the number of pieces of furniture in a small area.

it. And a desk is best sited in a place where it not only receives good light, but the light does not continuously reflect onto a computer screen. The same point is worth remembering when it comes to siting the television.

Choosing a sofa

Deciding on the fabric of your sofa is just a small part of choosing the actual piece. The next decision to make is the style. Although you may have already considered what sort of look you want, think about the practicalities of the design you choose as well. Do you tend to relax on the sofa alone or with your partner or children? If the whole family tends to gather there, you will need one that is large enough to cope but that will not dominate the small scale of the living room.

Good sofas for small rooms

☐ Low-backed designs enable your eye to wander over them, increasing the impression of space.

☐ Chaise longue designs offer seating space without bulk or a high back.

☐ Curved designs can offer greater flexibility when it comes to positioning, and they provide generous seating space without taking up a whole wall.

☐ Two-seaters can be practicable for the reasons given above (see page 69).

☐ Sofa beds offer the option of an extra spare bed (see Chapter 4 on bedrooms).

Choosing for comfort

Comfort is just as important as the style. Before you buy a chair or sofa, relax into it as you would at home. The upholstery should support you well, without sagging or being too rigid. The small of your back and your neck should be supported and the arms should be at a comfortable height. Does anyone in the family have a back problem or do you have an elderly person in the home? They certainly won't appreciate a design that slopes towards the back of the chair and is difficult to get out of.

Space-saving storage

Perhaps more than any room in the home the living room needs smart, effective storage. What you feel is acceptable to have on view and what is not is a matter of personal taste, but most living rooms require some shelf space for books, records and CDs, and hi-fi equipment, television, videos and so on.

Assess the storage potential of your living room. Older style buildings with chimney breasts have the added advantage of alcoves to either side, and these create perfect storage areas for day-to-day clutter. Make the most of these recesses by filling them with built-in shelf and storage units or carefully chosen pieces of slim-line, free-standing furniture, which will do the job for you and have the advantage of being portable when you move home.

Useful free-standing furniture for alcoves

Look especially for cupboard spaces that are large enough to conceal a television set or

A single piece of furniture could resolve many of your planning problems, so it is worth waiting until you find the piece you want or considering having one built specially for you. This antique piece offers both study and bedroom storage options in a design that is perfect for the traditional style of the room.

71

ROBERT DOISNEAU
Les enfants de la place Hébert, 1957
Centre National de la Photographie-Flammarion 4

Emphasize your room's best points to distract attention from the lack of floor space by making the most of architectural features, high ceilings or any other interesting quirks your room may have. Here the columns at either side of the door lead the eye up to the unusual ceiling, and wall-to-wall shelving draws attention to the full width of the room in an awkward alcove. A good balance of features at both high and low levels in a room will make it look more successful, and the high uplighters have been chosen to complement the low-level furniture.

A run of free wall space is often best used when it is fitted with a range of storage units. A closed front can conceal bulky items, such as a hi-fi, while an open front offers a place to display treasured items or books, and both provide an extra surface to work on. Fitted units can be made to look as traditional or modern as you wish.

hi-fi equipment. It is not difficult to drill holes through the back to allow access for the wires and it gives your living room a more streamlined finish. Also consider the following:

■ Desks and bureaux with fold-down writing areas and drawer or cupboard space.

■ Old-fashioned dressers, such as pot board or simple Welsh dressers, have good display shelves, combined with plenty of cupboard and drawer space.

■ Tall, slim-line chests of drawers are good for holding papers, CDs and tapes and so on.

■ Trunks and storage chests are useful for storing items that are not in everyday use as you are certain to cover the top with clutter, lighting or accessories. These lower items work best when shelves are added above them to provide extra height and storage.

Larger or fitted storage units

Although large units are clearly useful for the storage space they offer, be careful that they do not dominate a room. Opt for low, slim line designs where possible, and go for neutral, cool colours or a shade that blends with the surrounding walls so that it is as unobtrusive as possible. If the units incorporate pull-down tables, mini-bars or other useful concealed features, use your scaled floor plan to check that you will have room to open them out and use them comfortably before you commit yourself. Remember that it is likely that there will be more than one person in the room at the same time, wanting to use different pieces of furniture or to pass through, and you must take this into account at the planning stage.

Effective use of shelving

If you do not have the floor space for many storage units, turn to the walls for the shelf space they can offer. If you need wall-to-wall shelving to house an extensive library, use it. When you live in a small space, having a place to store everything takes priority. There is no need to sacrifice style completely however. Even floor to ceiling shelving can be artfully concealed with lengths of material made into curtains, fabric blinds or screens if you feel it is necessary. If the clutter you need to store is in desperate need of concealing, invest in coordinated storage boxes, such as decorated hat boxes, to streamline the look and turn an eyesore into a feature.

Smart side-tables

Side-tables are essential for making your living room a more comfortable place to be. They offer somewhere to rest a book, a drink or snack and also provide space for table lamps, flowers, a telephone and so on. A side-table should always be of a similar height to, or slightly lower than, the arm of the chair it is adjacent to, and when choosing side-tables for the small living room it is worth looking for the following:

■ Glass-topped tables appear to take up less space than more solid designs.

■ Fine-legged tables allow more of the surrounding space to be seen.

■ Designs incorporating a shelf below offer extra storage for magazines and books.

■ Folding tables and nests of table are flexible and useful for entertaining.

Flooring

Whatever surface you choose for covering your floor, it must be relatively hard wearing as well as smart. Your living room may be small, but it has to endure a lot of traffic, especially if you have children or entertain a lot, so you may as well assume from the start that whatever you use to cover the floor will come into regular contact with spills and boot polish. You will also, however, want a floor covering that is warm and comfortable, especially if you are relying on floor cushions for extra seating or have children who play on the floor a lot. So what is the solution? Well, it comes down to personal preference in the end, but here are a few of the options to consider.

Bare floorboards

Sanded and varnished or painted floorboards look very attractive, especially in period properties, and they will withstand plenty of wear. In a downstairs living room they can be draughty, however, so cover them with rugs – ideally ones that can be cleaned easily – for comfort and warmth.

Carpet

Carpet muffles sound effectively and softens the look of a room. In a small living room, a fitted carpet in a cool colour will effectively increase the impression of space as it takes the eye to the corners of the room. It also offers comfort and warmth underfoot. For extra practicality, opt for carpet with a relatively high content of man-made materials and a stain-resistant finish, rather than pure new wool. Alternatively, you could cover a more expensive neutral carpet with cheaper rugs to extend its life and offer more flexibility of colour scheme.

Natural flooring

Materials such as coir, seagrass and sisal have become increasingly popular as floor coverings for their natural beauty and durability. The light, natural shades are also useful for creating an impression of space. For a living room, however, it can still feel a little coarse underfoot, unless you opt for a more expensive wool mixture. The natural texture of the materials may be hard-wearing, but it is difficult to clean if you do have a lot of food and drink spills.

Sloping ceilings in a small room do not have to be restrictive, especially if you design your storage space around them. Glass-topped tables are a good choice for small rooms because they appear to occupy less space than they actually do. When they are used in living/dining rooms they can remain unobtrusive during the day, and become the centre of attention at night.

Lighting a small living room

The living room offers the greatest scope for choice of lighting than any room in the home. There is no longer any excuse to rely on one ceiling light – it is boring, flattening and unflattering, especially in a small room.

Once you have worked out your seating and furniture plan, make sure that you have enough sockets to light it adequately. As a rule of thumb, allow for a light source next to every seating space in the room, so that any-one reading, studying, watching television or just relaxing will be able to switch on an ad-equate level of lighting. Think about placing table lamps and free-standing lamps at the side of every sofa or armchair in order to achieve this, and consider adding wall lights for any areas where space is too tight to accommodate a lamp.

Lighting can be used in rooms of any size to highlight areas of particular interest, such as collections or displays, but in the small living room you can use lighting to your advantage to highlight items in the far corners, which will draw the attention of the eye to the furthest extent of the room and so increase the impres-sion of available space. Use picture lights or directed spot-lights to illuminate works of art on the walls, collections in glass-fronted cabi-nets, or an attractive piece of pottery displayed on a shelf. Pools of light around the room will add focal points if the room lacks them.

The narrowest rooms take on a completely new char-acter when one wall is covered in mirrored glass. The perceived space is doubled, and the glass helps to reflect light back into the room as well. If you decide to use mirrored glass from floor to ceiling, it can be even more effective if you place half-size items in front of it – console tables and half-size lamp-shades, for example – so that they become whole within the reflection. Remember to remove any skirting board or cornice on that wall, and end your carpet or tiling halfway through the pattern. The small-scale design of this tiled floor is a good choice for a small room, yet it is smart enough to suit the mock grandeur of the room.

Whatever the size of your room, make sure that every seating space has a lamp or light to one side of it to allow comfortable reading. If you do not have the floor space, use wall lights. Adjustable spot-lights in the ceiling highlight items of interest in the room to make the overall effect more dramatic, and a mirror helps to reflect extra light into the room.

Window dressing

When it comes to finishing your windows you need to consider several factors in addition to the finished look. In a living room you will want a design that looks smart and stylish, as befits a room that is most frequently on view to visitors, but any curtains you choose may also need to provide insulation if your windows are draughty, privacy if you are overlooked and be washable if you have children, pets or like to throw wild parties. As yours is also a small living room, you need to bear in mind that you don't want your window dressing to dominate the room, make it too dark or take up more wall space

than is essential. For these reasons, floor-length designs may not be appropriate because not only is this style of curtaining likely to be more full and bulky, but when the curtains are closed the curtaining will restrict the use of the space below the window, which could be more usefully used as a seating area or for another piece of furniture. Grand swags and tails are also likely to be unsuitable if you want to avoid the windows dominating the room completely. Instead, look for more restrained elegance, in the form of simple pelmets and valances, pinch, cartridge or box pleats, or more casual swags, achieved by wrapping fabric around a curtain pole. Don't

If your windows are small but you hanker after a grand effect, there is no reason you shouldn't achieve it. Fitting a curtain pole high above the window will ensure that a swag doesn't block out any light, and keeping the fabric width to a minimum at the sides reduces the amount of wall space the curtains need and prevents them from dominating the window.

discount Roman or even roller blinds. They can be dressed up with an impressive pelmet and you could trim them to match your furnishings to give a touch of sophistication.

Curtain tie-backs are always useful in the small living room because they allow as much light as possible to enter the room in daylight hours, as well as keeping curtains looking neat and tidy. Simple fabric tie-backs are easy to make yourself, while heavy cord and tassels can create an opulent look.

Another way of making sure that you allow as much light into the room as possible is to extend the pole beyond the window frame

and to draw back the curtains on it to its full extent. However, in a small room this does mean losing valuable wall space on each side of the window and it may make the window area appear disproportionately large for the scale of the room.

If privacy is a problem, look at ways of combining sheer fabrics with your heavier curtains. Muslin, voile and lace panels can all be hung from a lightweight track inside the window frame to allow light to filter through while protecting you from unwanted gazes, and they offer a more stylish alternative to standard net curtaining.

Small living rooms are, by their nature, often darker than they should be, so look at every way you can of allowing the light to flood in. A glazed door to the outside provides an extra light source and the curtains have been hung so that they can be pulled right away from the glazed area. Curtains need not hang on both sides of every window – drawing them back to one side only makes the wall space appear less cluttered and leaves it free for pictures.

Bench-style seating is ideal for narrow dining areas and could be a way of putting a narrow part of a room to good use. If you do not like the modern look, you could have traditional built-in seats fitted. Narrow church pews are ideal, too, if you can get your hands on them.

The combined living and dining room

If your living room also has to serve as your dining room, the space has to work twice as hard. The way you approach the design of a living/dining room depends very much upon your lifestyle, but essentially you must assess how often you will want to use the dining area and how many people you regularly need to seat. Also ask yourself how you like to enter-

tain. Do you tend to have formal dinners or are you happy to entertain on a more ad-hoc basis?

If you live alone and tend to eat in the kitchen or on your lap in front of the television, your living room space will be more important to you, and you will not need to have a table and chairs set up permanently for the purpose of dining. A round or drop-leaf table, which may be used more frequently as a study or lamp table, can be brought from the sidelines to centre stage whenever it is needed and dressed up with a smart cloth to look the part, while folding chairs or other chairs from around the home can be brought in for seating. It is chic and fashionable to offer a mixture of chair designs these days, so why not make the most of it and save the money otherwise spent on a matching dining suite that you would use only occasionally.

If you are happy to dine informally with friends, invest in a good sized coffee table, which can be placed between two sofas or in the middle of a collection of armchairs and laid for supper. Floor cushions are easily stored in small corners and under the bed to be brought in to offer extra seating.

If, however, your family eats together every evening or you entertain frequently, you need to allocate more permanent space for a dining table. In the combined living/dining room it may still be necessary to make use of a table that serves another purpose during daylight hours, so try to incorporate ample storage space into your room design so that the paraphernalia from the day can be whisked away and hidden until the morning. If, on the other hand, space is more precious during the day, consider a fold-away table

and chairs instead, because they can be left at the side of the room or even behind a sofa when they are not in use.

If you have the space for a permanent dining table and chairs, set about creating a separate mood and look for the dining room area to separate it visually from the living room. Flooring is always a good starting point. If you are intending to change the flooring in your room, consider opting for two different textures or colours to create a visual divide. If your living room area is to be carpeted, perhaps you could tile the dining room area or lay a wooden floor or strip and varnish existing floorboards, to make the area both smart and practical. If you don't want to change your existing carpeting or flooring, use a large rug to create a different look in one of the areas instead.

Look at your colour schemes and see if you can create a complementary, but slightly different look for the dining area. If this area is to be in an alcove or slightly set apart from the living room space, make the most of it. If your living area is decorated in shades of blue with accents of yellow to warm it up, why not reverse the scheme and paint your dining area yellow, with accents of blue?

Another way of effectively dividing the

two rooms is to use a screen, shutters, a curtain or a pull-down blind to create a cosy, intimate dining atmosphere. Screens can be bought ready-made or you could make your own design from MDF and either paint it or cover it in a fabric to complement your furnishings. Pull-down blinds can even be painted, stamped or stencilled with fabric paints so that they are left plain perhaps on the living room side, but present quite a different image to the people who are dining.

Lighting can also be used effectively to create a different atmosphere in the two areas. Candlelight is perfect for dining, and its adaptability also makes it a good choice for small space living. Turn the lights down low (or off) in the living room while you light candles on the table and around the dining area. Bulbs or candle-lit wall sconces are also perfect for illuminating the dining area. The most important rule is to make sure your lighting is flexible and, at all costs, avoid lighting the entire living/dining room area with just one overhead light. The two areas should work independently if possible.

Dual-purpose rooms or single-room apartments require especially careful placing of the furniture. This dining area is made quite separate from the seating space by turning the armchairs away from it. Arrange furniture in groups according to their function and invest in pieces that can work in more than one situation. This sideboard, for example, can be used for storing crockery and cutlery during the day, yet at night helps to bring the dining area to life by providing a surface for candles – the flames of which will be reflected in the mirror above.

6 The bathroom

Short on space, but not on style! Instead of being despondent about the limited area, why not flaunt it by making bold statements with colour and design. To imitate these creative touches you need to use an oil-based paint on the bathroom fittings and finish it with a waterproof varnish. Using a stencil will help you achieve the look you want if you don't have much confidence in your painting skills – and if you start with the toilet seat, you can always replace it if it goes wrong!

If you are struggling to see how you can make the best of a small bathroom, you can guarantee that you are not alone. Everyone would love to be able to luxuriate in good bathroom facilities, yet in most homes the bathroom remains the smallest room in the home. In smaller, older houses this is usually because the bathroom has been elevated from outside to inside status, and the owners no doubt felt at the time that this was a bold enough move without also sacrificing any more living space than was absolutely necessary. Yet even in modern properties, bathrooms have tended to remain small, either because of limited overall living space or because the demand for luxuries, such as a separate toilet or an *en suite* bathroom, has put increased pressure on the amount of floor space available.

Don't despair though. Like small kitchens, small bathrooms are often the most efficient of bathrooms, and you may be able to indulge yourself with more expensive tiling, wallpaper or units than you would otherwise be able to.

Perhaps it is a newly created *en suite* bathroom that you are now looking to style, and you are happy to accept any limitations imposed by its size because you have another bathroom somewhere else in the home. If so, that's fine, you can skip ahead to Decorating your bathroom (see page 95). Many people, however, will be looking for inspiration on how to transform their cramped family bathroom into something more stylish and practical. If you fall into this camp, but are lucky enough to have surplus space elsewhere (perhaps in the form of a rarely used guest room, a large adjoining bedroom or some extra landing space), now is the time to consider playing around architecturally to create the kind of bathroom you dream of.

If you have the space, adding a basin or shower cubicle in a larger bedroom would reduce the pressure in the bathroom at rush hours. Look at ways in which you might be able to re-site the bathroom completely or, for a less extreme solution, steal some space from an adjoining area to expand into. Knocking through and erecting new partition walls in a more appropriate place need not be as expensive as you might imagine, and it will make your day-to-day living – let alone your design decisions – far, far easier. Do, however, check your local building regulations in case you need approval before you make any major structural alterations.

If none of this sounds feasible, look at the space within the bathroom itself to see how it might be improved. The first thing to establish, as ever, is your budget. If cost is not an issue, there is no reason not to contemplate a complete redesign, including a new small-scale bathroom suite (see below for more details on your choice of fixtures and fittings) or a more practical layout. If this is the case, it would be worth calling in a few specialist

It might be worth employing the services of a carpenter to help you make the most of all available space. A bath panel such as this one, with a feature cupboard, isn't a standard length, but has been designed especially to offer a little extra concealed storage behind the bath – perfect for hiding the cleaner and bleach.

designers to see what ideas they have for your particular space. At the same time, of course, you should make your own room plan on squared paper and juggle with scaled-down versions of various suites to see what solutions you can come up with (see Chapter 1 for how to plan on paper). A registered plumber will be able to advise on any restrictions the existing plumbing system immediately imposes and which of your plans would be most cost effective. Some arrangements cost more than others to realize if they require a difficult or an uneconomic route for the necessary pipework.

When you juggle on paper with the various elements of your bathroom, allow yourself enough space between each piece so that using the bathroom is comfortable and practical. Here are some general guidelines:

■ Leave 80cm (31in) in front of a hand basin so that users are able to bend over.

■ Allow 80cm (31in) in front of a wc or bidet and 70cm (27in) at each side.

■ Maintain 80cm (31in) in front of the length of the bath for drying space and the same in front of a shower.

Choosing your bath
Size

To help get started with your planning, it is useful to know that, in Britain, standard baths are usually 1.7m (about 5ft 7in) long and 711mm (28in) wide, but smaller sizes are available, going down in gradations of 102mm (4in) in both length and width. Some hip baths are only 314mm (12in) long, but these mean that, in order to bathe, you sit on one level with your feet lower down, so you cannot stretch out.

The sides of a bath vary in height too, but although a design with lower sides may suit the scale of your room, consider who will be using it. Children find the lower sided baths easier to get in and out of (possibly soaking the floor in the process), while old people usually prefer to have a high side to hold onto.

Materials

Don't rule out a traditional tub for your small-scale bathroom. Antique free-standing baths are not easy to find and can be rather expensive, but they are not as large and bulky as you might imagine. The traditional tub design slopes in towards the end opposite the taps, so the free floor area is that little bit larger than it would be if you chose a panelled bath. Even the Victorians designed a few smaller style baths, such as the sitz-bath, which allowed you only enough space to sit while you bathed. Many of the old-fashioned designs can be installed almost anywhere in the room as they look good from all sides, so they do offer a certain amount of flexibility, which is, unfortunately, usually wasted in the small bathroom. These old baths also have the most hard-wearing finish, being made from cast iron and

Don't immediately dismiss the idea of a bath simply because space is tight. Shop around for specially made small tubs. This bathroom proves that you can create a sophisticated look in the smallest setting. Even an acrylic bath can be made to look grand if it is encased in wooden panels with decorative mouldings and adorned with smart taps.

A small family bathroom needs to be decorated practically as water will reach every corner at bath time. Tiled walls and floors are perfect – although they will be slippery underfoot for toddlers – and the corner bath arrangement makes it possible for two people to use the bathroom at the same time. Raising the bath helps to create an impression of greater space, which is emphasized by the cool blue-grey tiles.

enamelled with porcelain – reconditioned antique baths will probably have been given a new finish – but this does mean that the water cools down more rapidly, so they are not ideal if you like to linger in a hot bath.

New baths are usually made from acrylic and reinforced with glass fibre. They are lightweight and come in a wide range of colours and shapes, but they are susceptible to being scratched. These designs are finished with side and end panels, which are usually made from plastic or wood. Whichever material you choose, go for a colour that blends with or matches the bath itself unless you want to draw attention to the bulk of the bath.

Another option is, of course, the sunken bath, although it is usually possible only in ground-floor bathrooms, but it could be one way of opening up space in the room.

Taps

Think about where you would ideally like to have the taps positioned on your bath. If you or your children like to share a bath it may be better to choose a design with taps on one side or across a corner, so that one person doesn't run the risk of scalding themselves and is unable to lean back comfortably. This could also save you a few millimetres of precious space!

Showers

If the luxury of a bath is something you can live without, you could release a lot of valuable floor space by opting for a shower cubicle instead. A possible drawback is that future buyers may be deterred if there is no bathtub in the home, but children will still be able to bathe in it if you choose a design with a tray that is deep enough and it has a plug fitted instead of just a drain. Usually you will need an area of about 813 × 914mm (32 × 36in) to accommodate a shower tray.

Opening doors

The sort of shower doors or curtaining you use will have quite an impact on the look of your bathroom and the perceived amount of space, so choose carefully. Sealed shower doors have the advantage of being watertight, but when they are shut they can be quite imposing. Avoid darkly tinted glass and consider instead an etched or distorted glass design, which will offer a certain amount of privacy but allow the eye to pass through it more easily so that it appears to be less of a barrier and the room seems to be more open. From a practical point of view, it is better to avoid a door with ridges in the glass because they catch all the dirt.

Don't forget to think about the amount of space that is available when you look at how the shower doors open. A door that swings out into the room may cause problems if more than one person uses the bathroom at a time on busy mornings.

Another, more space-efficient, option may be to use one or more of your existing walls as the wall or walls of the shower area and front it with a curtain. When the curtain is drawn back to the side, it gives the impression that the bathroom has more available space than is the case, but it has the disadvantage of being less watertight, so your flooring would need to be suitably waterproof.

Bath/shower combinations

If you love soaking in the bath, but also enjoy the option for fast bathing offered by a shower or if your accommodation is fitted with a water meter and you want to conserve as much water as possible, consider combining the two. When space is short it is not practicable to try and squeeze a bath and a separate shower cubicle into one room, and installing a shower above one end of your bath is a workable alternative. Check that your plumbing arrangements will allow this kind of arrangement, and ideally choose a bath that has a flat, less rounded end below the shower fitting.

Do not be deterred if there is a window just where you want to attach a rail for a shower curtain. There are several very flexible curtain rail systems on the market, making it possible to create a structure that suits the most awkward angles and corners. Another solution would be to have a mosquito-net-style curtain falling from a circular frame, attached to the ceiling.

Hand basins

When it comes to choosing your hand basin, it will be a matter of juggling the priorities of space and needs. There are plenty of tiny corner hand basins that take up minimal space, but if you like to wash your hair in a basin or tend to splash around a lot as you shave in the morning, a small basin is not going to be practical – unless, that is, you have more space in another room, such as the bedroom, to incorporate a more suitably sized basin for those sort of activities.

A good compromise is to select a reasonable size of sink set into a vanity unit, so that a small area of the bathroom becomes not only a washing area but also a surface on which you can arrange attractive accessories with useful storage space below. A bonus is that the ugly pipework from the basin is concealed without the expense of a pedestal. If you are very lucky you may have room to fit two basins in one worktop unit, so that two people can brush their teeth or wash at the same time in the morning, making your bathroom space work doubly hard. Remember to

Vanity units are useful and stylish in a confined area, bringing a streamlined look to a small room and providing extra storage space for lotions and potions. This unit was selected to reinforce the traditional style of the window and tiles.

Prints are ideal for displaying in a tiny bathroom because they lie flush against the wall, instead of in frames, and the beautiful small-scale detail of old-fashioned prints can be more easily appreciated. Photocopy prints from source books, give them a wash with cold tea to age them, cut them out and stick them to the wall. A coat or two of waterproof varnish will protect them from splashes. Such a treatment needs a good backdrop, so paint your walls in a warm, deep colour.

allow ample arm room between the two sinks. You need about 70cm (27in) around a basin if you are using it to wash your hair.

Choosing a WC

Most lavatories now are made from hard-wearing vitreous china, but there is a wide range of different styles available. For your small bathroom consider the following:

■ Wall-mounted wcs release floor space but are rather heavy, so they need to be fitted to a sound wall; a partition wall is not suitable.

■ High-level cisterns, as favoured by the Victorians, look elegant and raise the eye upwards, creating interest at a higher level.

■ Slim-line cisterns can sometimes be fitted into the depth of the bathroom wall, making

them space saving as well as water efficient.

■ Cisterns hidden in a unit create a stream-lined look and perhaps an extra storage shelf on top of the unit.

Ventilation

Many small bathrooms, especially *en suite* arrangements and those in modern properties, do not have a window, so excellent ventilation is essential to prevent a build-up of condensation and black mould. You will need a powerful electric extractor fan, which is usually controlled by a light-pull cord.

Creating more space

If a new, more compact suite is out of the question, look at other ways of releasing the space in the room. Could anything in the room currently taking up valuable floor space be moved out or upwards, onto the walls? Are there any wasted areas that could be put to better use? Common places to consider are around the basin pedestal and the free wall space. Both of these areas might be used more efficiently as storage areas for cleaning materials, lotions and potions, or towels.

What sort of door does the bathroom have and how does it open? Would it make more sense to hang it the opposite way, either so that it opens into the other side of the room, or (if there is enough hall space) out onto the landing, or would a sliding or folding door be convenient?

Is a bulky radiator taking up valuable floor space? Why not change it for a wall-mounted heated towel rail to take it out of the way and at the same time make it more useful. Messy towels always let down any bathroom, so having somewhere to store them neatly when they are both dry and damp will instantly improve your bathroom's appearance.

Is ugly pipework running around the bathroom still visible? By boxing it in imaginatively you will not only make it look neater, you could also create a useful bench seat (perhaps with a lift-up lid for extra storage or a laundry basket) or a small cupboard.

Bathroom furniture

It is unlikely that you will be able to fit freestanding pieces of furniture into a small bathroom, but keep a look out for attractive wall-mounted or corner cupboards and any small pieces you think may fit the bill. Antique pieces (or cheap wooden furniture given an effective paint treatment) prevent the bathroom from becoming too clinical and add charm to a traditionally styled room.

Fitted units are well worth considering. Not only will they create plenty of concealed storage and open shelf space, but they will streamline the look of the room and create an effective space out of an awkward area. Do not be deterred by the thought that that they will look too modern for your taste. Fitted units can be made from natural woods or painted to give a traditional as well as a completely up-to-the-minute look. Consider running a row of fitted units along one wall of the bathroom at least, incorporating either the toilet or the hand basin into the design. They need not be very deep to be useful.

Other storage solutions
Shelving

Many bathroom accessories are so attractively packaged that they can be put on display, so make the most of spare wall space by fixing a

Fitted units will streamline the look of a small bathroom, while offering plenty of practical features within a confined space. Bathroom shelves don't need to be deep to store attractive bottles and soaps, so there's no excuse for not incorporating some shelving into your scheme.

Keep it simple is a good rule when you are designing for a small space. The Shakers knew how to create simple yet beautiful objects, so why not follow their example. Peg rails are a stylish way of providing extra hanging space and, because they can be fixed to walls almost anywhere and at any height, they are perfect for awkward spaces.

few shelves on which to store them. Glass shelves look attractive and are less obtrusive than other materials, but choose a material that will blend with the room's overall decoration.

Hooks and peg rails

Keep odds and ends tidy and off your valuable surfaces by hanging them from smart hooks or Shaker-style wooden peg rails. Buy or make coordinating drawstring bags to house knickknacks and clutter, hang them from pegs above the bath (the ideal place for

bags full of new soaps, shampoos and so on), along the wall or on the back of the door.

Boxes

Less attractive bits and pieces of bathroom paraphernalia, such as partly used make-up or shaving equipment, can be hidden in smart boxes or jars, so releasing shelf space and allowing you to carry them into another room if necessary. Cleaning materials can be stored in plastic crates and hidden in a cupboard or on a high shelf.

Mirrors are at their most effective when they cover a large expanse of wall, giving the impression that the whole wall is further from you than it really is. Consider where you could place a large sheet of mirrored glass to achieve the best results. The most obvious places include above the bath, running from one end of that wall to the other, or above the wash basin, again covering as much of the wall space as possible. Ideally, place two mirrors opposite each other so that they reflect into one another, defying anyone looking into them to establish where the walls actually begin and end. If you cannot achieve that, at least hang plenty of pictures or objects of interest opposite the mirror so that it can reflect something other than a boring blank wall.

If you can afford it, invest in heated glass so that it does not steam up while the bathroom is in use, or improve the ventilation by adding an extractor fan, even if you have a functioning window.

Emphasize the room's best features

A long, narrow bathroom will benefit if you use decorative techniques that emphasize its length. A line of decorative or contrasting tiles or a wallpaper border that runs the length of the room, for example, will make it appear to stretch further than it actually does.

Windows

Could any existing windows be enlarged to let in more light and open up the room? Is it possible to add another window, such as a skylight, if the bathroom is at the top of the property? If you cannot change the window, remove any window dressings that block out too much light and replace them with something simpler (see Window dressings, page 99).

Take a look at the quality of the glass in your existing windows. It may be better to get rid of old, thick obscured glass and to replace it with a more attractive modern etched design.

A perfect example of how mirrored glass can fool the eye and help you create space where there is none: you would almost believe there was a double basin in this bathroom. If you want to recreate this effect, try to avoid placing anything on the glass that will interrupt the reflection, such as these power points.

Creating the impression of space

The final line of attack in the battle against a small room is to adopt ways and means of creating an impression of space. Here are some suggestions.

Mirrors

Your most effective tool is mirrored glass. The bathroom is the one room in the home where you have got free rein when it comes to fixing mirrors. It is, after all, the room for washing and beautifying yourself, and mirrors are an essential part of the process. So how fortunate it is that mirrors can also add to the sense of light and space.

Glazed doors

Replacing a solid bathroom door with a glass-panelled design will allow more light to enter the room, and if you choose etched, frosted or even stained glass for the panels you need not sacrifice any privacy.

Colour

The selection of colours, not only for the bathroom suite, but also the walls and ceiling will have an instant effect on the perceived light a room receives and the impression of space. See Decorating your bathroom, below, and turn back to Chapter 2 on colour to refresh your memory on ways in which colour can work for you.

Decorating your bathroom

A bathroom, like a bedroom, can be the place you are able to indulge yourself when it comes to decoration. Because you do not have to spend all day there, you can be more frivolous about the decoration and even more daring than you would normally be. Consider who will be using the bathroom and what kind of impact you want the room to have. Is it a bathroom that visitors will use? If so, you may want to provide plenty of amusing, interesting or pretty accessories for them to enjoy. Is it a private *en suite* bathroom? If so, you can make a truly personal, luxurious haven. Perhaps it is a bathroom that children use, when you will want to make it bright and fun. Or is it a room that is used by everyone, when you will want to make it look stylish but not somewhere people will choose to linger for too long.

The secret, whatever finish you want, is to make sure that the same style or 'look' is continued throughout, from your choice of taps to your light fittings. In a small bathroom every inch of space has to work for you, and if you forget to pay attention to details, the finished scheme will not be as effective as you had hoped.

Once you have decided on the style of bathroom you want or the theme you want to impose, you need to choose the right colours and materials to suit the space you are working in. If you have to work around an old suite, you may be limited in your choice of colour. Do not feel too restricted, however. Covering up the bath with new panels, which can be painted, and fitting a unit around the basin and even the cistern will create a new look and distract attention from the existing colours.

If the existing tiles look out of place with your plans, consider replacing them. The advantage of having a small bathroom is that it may not be too expensive to re-tile the whole room. If the tiled areas suffer little wear and tear, consider painting them with eggshell or gloss paint to blend with your new scheme.

Do not be afraid to go for warmer, more dramatic colours in a small bathroom. It is sometimes more effective to emphasize the cosiness of a room and even its more awkward architectural features. If you like to laze in a foam-filled bath every evening, deep blue, warm green or even rich red will look most effective by candlelight. Choose a colour that will suit the light your bathroom receives, and then decide how 'dark' you are prepared to go. If you want people to get in and out of the bathroom quickly, a cool shade, such as mint green or pale blue, will keep them on their toes! And if you can't make up your mind about a colour scheme and your bathroom receives enough natural light, plain white always looks fresh and appealing. Bear in mind that in a north-facing room, however, it may end up looking somewhat grey.

Whatever colours you choose, go for practical finishes. Wallpaper should be vinyl and paint should be oil based. Avoid using paint of any kind around areas frequently exposed to water, such as by the bath, shower or basin, because it will soon show signs of wear. Tiles are ideal for these areas and are available in a wide range of colours and designs.

Fixing lights on or around your bathroom mirror provides good illumination for putting on make-up or shaving. Boxing in a radiator not only streamlines the appearance of the wall but provides an extra shelf, while an awkward bit of wall has been used for a towel rail. Green and white are good choices for small rooms because green is from the cooler, receding half of the colour wheel.

Lighting

Just because your bathroom is small, you should still get away from having just one light hanging from the centre of the ceiling. This kind of light is not flattering to your decoration, and it certainly will not be flattering to you if you want to use the bathroom mirrors for shaving or making up. To provide an attractive and practical combination of accent and task lighting, focus on fittings that will cast a general glow of light around the room and add specific fittings for the basin and mirror area. Remember that, for safety, all your lighting should be controlled from outside the room or by a pull-cord.

Whatever type of light fittings you choose, don't forget to have some candles on hand to create a soft, romantic and relaxing atmosphere when you want it. If your bathroom is so small you don't have any free surfaces on which you can stand candles, consider fixing one or two candle sconces to the walls around the bath.

Flooring

In a small bathroom it is best to keep the design of your flooring as plain and simple as possible. A small floor will be overwhelmed by fancy designs. So, if you yearn for a spread of dramatic geometric tiles, try to resist the urge until the day you have a larger space at your disposal. There are plenty of finishes to choose from in the meantime.

The best floor finish should be both practical and suit the style of your bathroom. In a modern city bathroom a sleek, luxurious finish will complement chrome and shiny tiles, so choose ceramic tiles (if your floor is solid enough), marble, or a smart linoleum or vinyl. If your bathroom has a more traditional or cottage style, consider bare boards (sealed with yacht varnish), slate, stone or sealed cork tiles. All these finishes will be practical and durable, although some (especially wood and cork) are less waterproof than others and you should also use a bath mat or rug to absorb any splashes when you bathe.

For general lighting in the bathroom choose at least one of the following:

- Recessed ceiling lighting: this is especially good for bathrooms with low ceilings, but make sure that the fittings are in sealed units that will protect the bulbs from water and condensation. You will have a choice of fixed-position bulbs or adjustable eyeball designs.

- Wall lights: when they are fitted above eye-level, these will provide a softer effect than recessed spot-lights and, as they come in a variety of styles, from traditional to contemporary, you will find one to suit your bathroom's mood.

For practical lighting around the basin area, consider one of the following:

- Tungsten strip lighting: if it is fixed behind a pelmet above the mirror, to prevent the light from glaring in your eyes, tungsten strip lighting is ideal for the bathroom. Do not confuse tungsten with fluorescent lighting, which casts an unflattering, harsh light; tungsten emits a warm, more yellowy light and, in strip form, is protected from condensation.

- A track of halogen bulbs around the mirror: these are perfect for getting an accurate picture of your face, without shaded areas. Low-voltage halogen light is white and crisp, so it makes fittings sparkle. Buy bulbs with a special shield to protect them from the steam and have the necessary transformer fitted by a specialist.

Tiny windows look best
when they are simply
dressed, especially in a
bathroom. A sheer curtain,
topped with a pretty fabric
pelmet, is all that is needed
to provide privacy and
soften the edges of the
frame.

Carpeting is warm underfoot, but it is not always practical. If you must have carpeting, choose a type that is recommended for bathrooms and, again, use a rug to soak up any splashes.

Window dressings

Many small bathrooms do not have a window at all or, if they do, it is so small that it hardly seems worth bothering with. Most windows will, however, be improved if the frame is softened by the addition of some sort of dressing. Insulation is usually not an issue when curtains are chosen for the bathroom, because it is unlikely that they will ever be closed. In addition, because most bathroom windows are glazed with a suitably tinted, frosted, etched or distorted glass, privacy will not be an issue (if your bathroom glass is clear, however, see below). Essentially then, your only restrictions are in matters of style and light.

Assuming that you want to allow as much light as possible into a small bathroom, it would be sensible to avoid full or fancy curtaining, and this is especially true if you and your family tend to create quite a splash when you have a bath. Water travels surprisingly far in a small room, and expensive curtaining will not be improved by regular soakings. Full curtaining will also restrict the amount of light that is allowed into the room.

Consider softening the window with a simple dress curtain, such as a length of lace or muslin draped softly over a pole, or hung from curtain clips and gathered to one side.

If your bathroom is overlooked through clear glass, you can still gain a certain amount of privacy by using plenty of fabric and draping it so that it covers most of the window area.

A little café curtain suspended from a brass rod will also offer partial privacy, and give a fresh, country cottage look to a tiny attic bathroom window. Another solution would be to cut a panel of pretty lace to the size of the window frame and tack it to the frame to gain complete privacy and yet allow light to filter through.

If you prefer a sleeker, more minimalist look, a simple blind may be the answer. Made from a light-filtering fabric, such as a lightweight cotton, a blind can be kept partially drawn, and the edge trimmed to add decoration and interest.

For other ways of framing a small window without blocking out any light, look at the area around the window. Would the window suit shutters, permanently held back to the sides? Is there room to edge the whole window with a frame of decorative ceramic tiles? Would some simple dress curtains, which need not be full enough to close, do the job just as well?

If the window is architecturally interesting, don't be afraid to leave it alone, so that its form can be appreciated. If it is unusual or especially interesting, consider making it into a feature, with the help of a surrounding paint effect. A round window could become a porthole, a lifebuoy or an octopus's head, for example. Lie back in the bath and wait for inspiration to come!

7 The kitchen

If you do not have the space for storage cupboards at ground level, look upwards. Walls and ceiling are wasted if they are left bare while your cupboards are bursting. Fitted with shelves, racks and hooks, they will make your kitchen a more practical place and help to ensure that everything is to hand.

The kitchen is often referred to as the heart of the home, conjuring up images of families gathering around the range and children playing around the kitchen table, while friends linger in comfy chairs dotted around the room. Unfortunately the small kitchen is never going to fulfil this type of dream, and you need to approach the design of this area in a very practical way, with ergonomics, not family scenes, at the forefront of your mind.

Looking at it positively, the small kitchen is likely to be a more efficient work space than a vast room may ever be because everything you need will be close to hand and you will not have to work too hard to make sure that the hob, sink and preparation areas are close to each another. If you have ever seen a professional chef at work in a restaurant's small kitchen, you will know that it is certainly possible to produce cordon bleu dishes in the most confined of areas.

The questions you need to ask yourself before planning the room should focus on your cooking and eating habits, so that you can form an accurate picture of how you will want to use the space on a daily basis. If necessary, turn back to Chapter 1 to remind yourself of the most pertinent questions. People who tend to eat out rather than cook for themselves, for example, will need far less storage space for food and cooking utensils than someone who enjoys entertaining or cooks for a family every day. One person may put a small eating area, such as a breakfast bar, high on the list of priorities for the kitchen, while someone planning for a family might value space for a dishwasher or a large fridge-freezer far more highly. Only you can accurately assess your personal or family needs. Generally, however, the following will be required, to some extent or other:

- Food storage space
- Sink and drainer
- Food-preparation area
- Storage space for utensils and gadgets
- Cupboard for cleaning equipment
- Cooker and hob
- A washing-machine
- Storage space for crockery and cutlery
- Dustbin/waste disposal facilities

The following may be luxuries or basics, depending on your lifestyle:

- Eating area
- Dishwasher
- Microwave

Unfortunately, deciding on your basic requirements is only half the battle – in fact the challenge has only just begun! Making the most of the available space in a small

This kitchen window is ideally situated overlooking the garden with the sink underneath, allowing enjoyment of the view while washing up. Small windows are best left plain or dressed simply to allow maximum light to enter the room and to prevent the curtains from becoming a fire hazard. Choose washable fabrics, such as cotton, or spongeable blinds. If you want extra privacy at night you could fit a roller blind behind an attractive pelmet.

kitchen is like trying to complete a complicated jigsaw puzzle, and just when you think that you have nearly finished, you realize that one essential piece isn't going to fit into the space you had originally planned. When you are trying to incorporate standard-sized units into your kitchen space, working around existing sockets and radiators tends to be the least of your problems – you soon discover that doors and windows are in the wrong place, too. However, this will at least encourage you to focus on the existing lay-out, and question whether you should make more major changes – such as altering the position of a window or adding a hatch through to another room. Now is the time to do it and, when you are redesigning a small, awkward kitchen, it can make more sense to alter the original structure than to keep trying to fit a quart into a pint pot. In fact, if moving a window also allows you to work with standard-size units (rather than having a kitchen custom made), it may even save you money.

Creating a window

If you live in a house or ground-floor apartment, the best place for a window is usually overlooking the garden, with the sink under it, so that you can enjoy the view while you wash up or keep an eye on children as they play. If you spend a lot of time in the kitchen it may be worth moving the window to a different position or even having an extra window built exactly where you want it.

Playing with doors

When space is tight, the internal door to the kitchen may be better turned, to open out into the hall. You might even want to consider removing the door completely and having the doorway as an arch or using a curtain or sliding door. If you are concerned about cooking smells travelling throughout your home, replace a solid door with a glass-panelled design so that you allow maximum natural light into the room and increase the impression of space once the door is closed.

If your kitchen leads onto a garden or roof terrace, consider moving your back door so that it opens directly onto the garden or terrace, instead of the side access. In summer the garden can be treated as an extension of the kitchen, creating an extra dining area and somewhere to entertain guests. If you are planning structural changes, it might be worth considering French doors, which can be opened out onto a patio or terrace area beyond.

Another way of adding light and creating an impression of extra space, in the summer months at least, is to change a solid back door to a stable design, so that you can pin back the top half whenever it is warm enough. This style is particularly suitable for traditionally designed kitchens, but it is a fun and practical feature in any kitchen.

A glass door that leads outside is useful when you want to create an impression of extra space because the eye is naturally drawn out to the view beyond. Before you invest in a new door, think carefully about how it will affect traffic around the room when it is open. If your kitchen is small and busy, it is vital that movement is not impeded. This sliding door was the best option to prevent the open door restricting access inside or out.

Other door positions to consider are those that link the kitchen with your dining area inside the home. If the dining room is next to the kitchen, it might be more suitable to create an access directly from the kitchen to the dining area. Serving food will be easier and you will feel less cut off from family or guests sitting in that room while you work. A partly or fully glazed door between the two rooms would increase the impression of space, although you may prefer to be able to shut a solid door on the piles of washing up!

A further option is to install a small serving hatch or to knock an opening above kitchen unit height into the dining room so that the rooms are, to all intents, separate, but both can gain from the extra light and ease of access whenever necessary. A curtain or shutter doors across the gap will keep the rooms divided when the dining room is not in use.

A hatch or opening in part of the wall allows the cook to stay in contact with the guests. If your dining room is next to a small, dark kitchen, consider knocking through in this way to open up the two rooms. If you live in an open-plan apartment, a partition wall such as this will help to define the two areas as having separate functions without losing the overall impression of space.

There is no reason you should clutter up your limited workspace when you can always find room on a wall. Appliances such as a microwave can be housed on a sturdy shelf, and a high position for a cookbook holder saves your books from splashes and stains. A kitchen designed in this way, although small, works very efficiently, with everything close to hand.

Planning the layout

Once you have decided on any major structural changes, you need to plan how best to position the kitchen basics. Call in two or three kitchen designers and see what ideas they come up with for organizing your space efficiently. Not only are they used to coming up with solutions for small spaces, they are also likely to have computer aided design on their side (which makes the job much quicker and easier) and a knowledge of the range of space saving unit designs now available.

When you are planning the positioning of

the various elements of your kitchen it helps to be aware of the official recommendations for the amount of space you should allow between units and so on to make the most of the amount of space available while ensuring that you can work and move around the room comfortably. Ideally, the passage space between your units should be at least 1.25m (about 50in) if two people are likely to be in the kitchen at the same time. If the kitchen is more likely to be used by one person the majority of the time, you can reduce that width to about 75cm (30in).

A sliding door to a larder in a small kitchen means that access to other parts of the kitchen is not impeded while the door is open. The uniformity of the decorating scheme helps to create a sleek, integrated look, encouraging the eye to pass to the far sides of the room and thus appreciate the full extent of the space available.

These guidelines will take into account the amount of room needed when cupboard doors are opened, but don't forget to think about the way in which not only unit doors, but also the fridge and oven doors open. Most new models now offer the option of having the door hung to either side to suit the layout of your kitchen, but it may be better to avoid ovens with pull-down doors as they take up a lot of valuable traffic space when they are open. Think carefully, too, about your choice of unit fronts. In a very confined or awkwardly shaped kitchen it may be better to dispense with the idea of conventional door fronts and opt instead for roll-up, pull-down fronts, sliding doors, very narrow hinged doors or even just curtains run on a pole.

Wall cupboard units can be positioned about 400mm (16in) above your worktop, with the highest shelf less than about 1.7m (5ft 6in) high for comfortable access.

Work space

Work surfaces are something there will never seem to be enough of. You will want somewhere to drop the shopping bags when you come through the door, somewhere to prepare meals, somewhere to pile dirty crockery by the sink and somewhere to keep basic items such as your toaster and kettle to hand. Unfortunately, the small kitchen is unlikely to offer any of these areas without some careful planning, flexibility and a bit of imagination.

Fitting permanent worktop space to either side of your hob and sink should be a

Pull-up, pull-down cupboard doors are a good choice when you need to keep gangways clear at all times, and continuing a worktop round and into the room provides extra workspace, as well as creating a clear demarcation in an open-plan kitchen/dining area.

When space is at a premium, every extra work surface is useful, so look at ways of incorporating temporary pull-out or fold-down surfaces, which can do double-duty as a breakfast bar area, especially if they are combined with folding stools or chairs that can be kept out of the way when they are not in use.

priority, to make the basic functions of cooking and washing up trouble free. You may have to be prepared to regard additional preparation areas as being available only on a temporary basis in order to keep your kitchen as efficient and uncluttered as possible. Look to add extra worktops by incorporating one or more of the following pieces:

■ A fold-down worktop/breakfast bar: attaching a drop-down worktop to a spare wall may allow traffic through the kitchen to flow more freely on a regular basis, while at the same time offering space to prepare meals or have a snack whenever you need it.

■ A pull-out work surface: some kitchen

units have a small, pull-out section that can be used to extend the working area.

■ A butcher's block/butler's trolley: look for a design on castors that you can move to wherever you need it and then wheel it out of the way afterwards. If this item is going to work hard for you, choose a model with drawer space and hanging space for utensils, a knife block at one end or perhaps an extendable worktop.

■ A folding butler's tray: although this is likely to be too low to be regarded as a regular solution to the worktop problem, a butler's tray is a useful piece for the small kitchen, even if it is just somewhere to pop ingredients while you are cooking. The folding frame means that it can be stored flat against the wall when you are not using it and the tray top allows the surface to be lifted off and moved, or used as a tray, when necessary.

Storage space

Something else that you can never have too much of but that the small kitchen often sadly lacks is storage space.

If you are investing in new units, search out designs that offer clever hidden storage devices, such as carousels, which will allow you to store plenty of groceries in a limited space by swivelling the shelving space around so that you have easy access to everything. Cupboards fitted with pull-out wire baskets or shelves on runners also make it quick and easy to see what's what, and even the smallest of gaps can be covered with a door front to conceal slimmer items such as ironing boards or bottles.

If you are working with existing units, look out for clever plastic accessories, of the kind often available in hardware stores or specialist kitchen shops, which allow you to organize your cupboards more efficiently. Items which are particularly useful include plastic cupboard plate racks, which make it possible to stack plates in your cupboards in a more accessible way.

Don't forget open shelves. Use your cupboards to conceal the more unattractive kitchen bits and pieces and display the rest of your kitchen paraphernalia on open shelves, which can be fitted into even the tiniest spaces and, if you splash out on sets of attractive storage jars for groceries such as pasta, rice, cereal and flour, as well as the more usual tea, coffee and biscuit sets, the final look will be tidy and smart.

If you are planning a kitchen with a country look, positioning an open shelf unit above a small run of units can also help to create the impression of a Welsh dresser,

while taking up far less space than such traditional pieces usually demand. To complete the farmhouse look, add a row of cup hooks along the front of the shelves and use both the hooks and the shelves to display your prettiest pieces of china.

Wall hooks/racks

Pots and pans and kitchen utensils can make quite attractive displays when they are hung from wall hooks and will help to free up your cupboard space. Stainless steel accessories and shiny copper-bottomed pans are particularly effective – and it's an incentive to wash up extra carefully!

Buying a fitted kitchen can be the best way to make the most out of your space, so shop around to see which companies offer the best range of space-saving devices and have the most imagination when it comes to designing your room. Look out especially for carousel storage units, narrow or bi-folding doors and pull-out units that usefully employ otherwise redundant space.

A good way of making a feature from open shelving is to divide it into smaller areas. This approach works well in a confined space because it suits the dimensions of the room, as well as making a more attractive and efficient display. Alternatively, you could always design your shelving as a mixture of large and small cubes.

Suspended hanging space

The batterie de cuisine can be kept to hand when hung from an attractive ceiling attachment. Contemporary kitchens demand a gleaming stainless steel or cast iron circular rack, whereas country-style kitchens are better suited to the traditional wooden clothes airer, which, when hung with steel hooks, can carry plenty of kitchen utensils.

Plate racks

A stylish way of keeping plates stored neatly, a wooden or chrome plate rack placed above the kitchen sink also makes it quick and easy to tidy up when you've done the washing up. You don't even have to dry the plates! Look for a plate rack that is large enough to hold the amount of plates you use daily – or at least your most presentable designs!

Decorating the small kitchen

Small kitchens look most effective when they are given a unified look, rather than being made up of a hotch potch of door fronts, units and appliances. This doesn't necessarily mean that you have to opt for a fitted kitchen (although they do tend to be more space efficient). If you prefer the thought of investing in free-standing pieces that you can take with you when you move, that's fine, but buy pieces made from the same wood or given the same finish, and consider positioning the lower pieces beneath a made-to-measure worktop (it could be a wood to match the pieces you have chosen) to unite the look and provide more practical preparation space.

Another benefit of opting for fitted units or off-the-peg door fronts, is that white appliances such as dishwashers and washing machines can be hidden behind a run of unit doors to finish the integrated look.

If you cannot afford to replace your existing units, take heart. Painted furniture is very fashionable at the moment, and it is easier than ever to streamline the look of your kitchen by painting the various elements of it the same colour. You can even give a white fridge and your tiles a splash of colour, as long as you use a sufficiently tough paint, such as gloss. However, an increasing number of manufacturers are recognizing the return to colour and bringing out a range of brightly coloured fridges and freezers, so you may find a new one to suit your scheme.

When you are lacking in storage cupboards below, use the space up above. Wall racks are not only practical for hanging your batterie de cuisine, they can become attractive features in their own right.

Stainless steel is making a comeback in the kitchen. It is practical for worktops, looks stunning and, in a small dark kitchen, helps to reflect the light rather than absorbing it as dark wood does.

Practical finishes

All kitchens, whatever their size, need to be decorated in tough, practical finishes, but in the small kitchen this is even more important, chiefly because any surfaces you do have will need to be multi-purpose and be able to withstand whatever you throw at them, but also because a small area, which inevitably gets a lot of traffic, is bound to suffer more than its fair share of bumps and scuffs. There is no room in the small kitchen for delicate surfaces and finishes.

The best work surfaces will withstand chopping with sharp knives, hot pots and pans and abrasive kitchen cleaners. Corian and laminated work surfaces are particularly good. Wooden surfaces must be well sealed and protected to be efficient. Tiles can be damaged, but they have the additional problem that the grouted gaps tend to attract crumbs and dirt, making them difficult to keep clean.

Tiles are, however, ideal for splash-backs behind the sink and along the back of your work surfaces, because they are water resistant and need nothing more than a wipe with a cloth to be kept looking good. The same can be said for a rather overlooked material – stainless steel sheeting – which always looks luxurious, yet is very easy to keep clean.

The kitchen walls must be given a tough and practical finish. Oil-based eggshell or vinyl silk emulsion paint are the best paint finishes to choose as they resist water and can be wiped clean. Look out for paints specially recommended for bathrooms and kitchens as they contain condensation resistant qualities. Wallpaper can also be effective, and can help to soften the look of a fitted kitchen, but choose a vinyl paper with a water-resistant seal.

Kitchen colour schemes

Your final choice of colour scheme will depend on your personal preferences as well as on the amount and type of light your kitchen receives (see Chapter 2), but most small kitchens benefit from being decorated with colours that are bright, fresh and cheerful, such as yellows and greens, with, perhaps, some dashes of red. The kitchen should be a welcoming and stimulating place, to cheer you up when you come down in the mornings and to keep you alert while you prepare the evening meal.

The colours of the worktop and tiles should also be chosen on the basis of practical considerations. These areas are going to be subjected to a multitude of foodstuffs and, although you will obviously need to keep your kitchen quite scrupulously clean, it is easier to live with a worktop that doesn't scream for a scrub every time someone puts down a cup of coffee or spills a drop of tea. For this reason, bright white worktops are probably best avoided, unless you like to spend all your time armed with the bleach.

Flooring the kitchen

Any flooring you choose will have to withstand constant splashes of water and hot fat or oil, crumbs, food stains, general spills and, if your kitchen leads to a garden, possibly wet or muddy feet. Carpet is unlikely to be the best choice, unless it is extremely heavy duty and stain resistant. Look instead at tougher coverings, such as tiles, brick, slate, wood or wooden laminated flooring, vinyl or linoleum. Each material has its benefits and drawbacks: tiles, brick and slate are cold under foot and anything you drop onto them is likely to shatter, but at least they can be thoroughly washed down; wood offers more warmth underfoot, but needs to be regularly maintained; good quality wooden laminate flooring will not dent or mark, but will not appreciate being soaked with water when it is cleaned; and the new 'natural' floorings such as sisal and coir matting tend to attract and retain crumbs and foodstuffs in their textured surfaces.

Don't skimp on kitchen lighting just because your room is small – a kitchen is a workshop and needs to be lit efficiently. A combination of adjustable spotlights and worktop lights, recessed under the wall units, works well.

Lighting the kitchen

The kitchen has to be considered as a working area and lit so that you can carry out your tasks there efficiently and without straining your eyes. However, it also needs to be considered as a living space, where over-bright pools of light may not be welcome, so it helps to make your lighting as flexible as possible (also see the section on lighting in Kitchen/dining rooms below). Maximize your sources of natural daylight, incorporating a new window or glazed door as suggested earlier if that is possible.

However small your kitchen, there is no excuse for being lazy about your lighting. Even if you have only one food preparation area it should be well illuminated by something other than, or in addition to, a simple central light. Tungsten tube lighting, fitted under the overhead cupboards or behind a pelmet, is ideal for highlighting a work surface, with directed spot-lighting coming a close second. Your hob may have a hood with its own lighting for illuminating the hob area as you cook, but if it does not, a directed spot-light will do the job here.

For a sleek, smart look investigate whether it is possible to fit recessed lighting between the joists of your kitchen ceiling for your overhead lighting – the overall effect is worth the effort and creates an even distribution of bright light, which is harder to achieve with spot-lights. If this is not possible, look at long tracks fitted with adjustable mini spot-lights. The more lights you have on the track, the more effective your lighting will be. In a kitchen you need to avoid leaving any areas badly lit, and the typical cluster of three spot-lights cannot cover all corners of even the smallest of rooms.

Kitchen/dining rooms

Adding a breakfast bar to your run of kitchen units is an easy way of including a casual eating area in the room, but creating a more formal dining area in your kitchen space is a challenge. This is largely because you need to combine what is essentially a work space with an area for relaxing and entertaining, while maintaining the right atmosphere in each – and making both areas work effectively. If the space you are working with is L-shaped, or divided in some distinct way into two areas, it makes the job much easier. If not, you need to rely on clever lighting and decorating effects to create the appropriate division or you may wish to consider ways of incorporating a more concrete visual divide.

Creating a divide

The advantage of a combined kitchen/dining room is that you can prepare food and chat to your guests at the same time – so the cook never misses out on the party fun! It's worth remembering this when you are thinking about ways of creating a division between the two areas, and limiting any physical barriers between the areas to something no taller than waist height, so that food can be easily passed over and conversation can continue.

When you are decorating an open-plan area try to maintain some continuity throughout so that the eye is naturally led around the room. At the same time, incorporate a few subtle changes to suggest the different functions of the various areas to help create a balanced, harmonious look that is easier to live with, too. The wooden floor of this living area is echoed in the wooden worktops of the kitchen, and the kitchen has been decorated in warm shades to stop it from looking too clinical and distinct from the rest of the room.

An ideal divide is a work-station or kitchen unit that can double as a food preparation area and a sideboard. It could be one that is permanently positioned as such, or it could be a work-station on castors, which can be moved to the centre of the room and back again when necessary. If it is a more permanent feature, aim to decorate it so that the side facing into the dining area is appropriate to an area of relaxation and the kitchen side offers more practical storage.

Another alternative is to add a partition wall of roughly unit height between the two areas. A work unit or shelving could be placed in front of it on the kitchen side and, if space is particularly short, bench seating could be attached or placed flush to the wall on the dining room side.

A more subtle divide

If a permanent, vertical room divider is out of the question, set about other ways of creating a subtle division between your two areas. Turn once again to Chapter 5 for suggestions on making a dining area out of a living space, and also consider the following suggestions.

Think about creating a divide with your choice of floor covering. Perhaps the small dining corner could be given a floor covering that is different from the rest of the kitchen floor to soften its look. Vinyl or tiles may be practical for the kitchen, but they are not as seductive in the dining room. It may be possible to carpet a small corner of the room, or at least to lay a rug under and around the table and chairs.

Use pattern, colour and texture to create a different look for your dining area. The plain painted walls of the kitchen could be given a more elegant stripe around the table, or paint could turn to wallpaper. You may even be able to add a dado rail at one end of the room or a decorative wallpaper border.

If there is a window at the dining end of the room, treat it more softly than those in the kitchen when you come to select a window dressing or curtaining style. Kitchens rarely lend themselves to curtaining, blinds being a more practical option in an area subject to water and naked flames, but the dining area window needs to be given the character that only gathers of fabric can offer. Choose a fabric that complements the kitchen blinds (or whatever dressing your other windows have been given), but allow yourself to be slightly more flamboyant in your choice of style and heading.

Light effects

When the dining area is in use and the cook is relaxing, it is important to be able to switch off the bright overhead lighting in the work area and create a soft, romantic atmosphere over and around the table, and this also helps visually to separate the dining area from the kitchen. When you plan your lighting for the kitchen, think about where the dining table is going to be placed and what sort of lighting effect you want around it. Remember to make sure that the lights in the dining area are controlled by a separate switch to those in the kitchen area.

An overhead light, controlled by a dimmer switch, which can be lowered to an intimate level above the table and raised again afterwards, is a flexible choice, giving you extra control over the amount of light the bulb casts into the room. Alternatively, you could opt for wall lights, and supplement the level of illumination with candles on and around the table. The small kitchen/dining area is unlikely to have space for extra furniture on which to place table lamps, but free-standing floor lights may be an option, if they can be tucked into a corner, away from the movement of chairs. Be careful when you site any of your floor or wall lights, though, that the shade doesn't cast the glare from the light bulb into the eyes of your diners.

If you live in a one-room apartment, try to think of the space as being divided into separate room sets, and position the furniture accordingly. Adding a rug and a splash of colour in the living area helps to soften the look in that corner, while open shelving and a half-height wall separate the kitchen area.

8 Halls, stairways and connecting spaces

The hall is the first – often the only – part of your house that visitors see, so it should be as welcoming and smart as possible. Not all hallways are as large or impressive as this one, but the smallest hallway could benefit from the treatments used here. Consider opening up your doorway with attractive glazing to allow the light to flood into your home, and use wall mirrors to reflect any extra light. If there is room, add some small-scale pieces of furniture, such as a console table, which will add interest and extra surfaces, without taking up a lot of precious room.

It is easy to overlook the hallway and stairs when you are designing and decorating your home, especially if they are rather cramped and small. Yet the hall is the place that visitors see first and the place from which they gather their first impression of your home, so it should be the part of your home where you pull out all the stops.

Halls are essentially areas of traffic, designed to make access to all parts of the home easy, and that should remain your prime consideration when you assess the potential of the area. There may be enough space to make the hallway of more use to you than as a simple corridor, but whatever adjustments and additions you make should not impede easy access to the other rooms. That said, there is still plenty that can be done to improve not only the look but also the efficient use of many halls and landings.

Most people make only a few demands on their halls, but they usually include the following:

- Hooks for coats
- Somewhere to drop keys, post and parcels
- A place to store wet umbrellas
- A looking-glass for last-minute checks

In small hallways this will probably be the most you can offer anyway, and in some very small homes even this can be a challenge.

Keep everything to an appropriate scale for the space available though, and you will manage to incorporate far more than you imagined possible.

Space for coats

If the space in your hallway is very tight it will be best to limit the hanging space to a couple of wall hooks to prevent vast numbers of outdoor coats from accumulating and taking up valuable room as well as looking untidy. Old-fashioned, free-standing, circular coat and hat stands are ideal for tight corners and usually offer space for umbrellas too. You could also look out for the somewhat bulkier, but useful, stands that incorporate a mirror. Houses often have understairs cupboard space, and this can be put to good use as a cupboard for coats. If you have room to position a few coat hooks inside the cupboard, the inside of the cupboard door can be left free for a full-length mirror.

Creating a surface

A hall table is an invaluable place for mail and keys as you come through the door and for leaving messages to other members of the family. It is also the ideal place to position a welcoming vase of fresh flowers or display a collection of pretty accessories to add interest to the area.

In many small halls, however, a table would become more of an obstacle than an advantage, so look for other ways of incorporating a table space instead. Fixing a narrow shelf to a wall is one way of doing this that also creates the impression that the hall is wider than it is, because it draws the eye to the sides of the area, allowing it to appreciate the full width of the space. Another method is to fix a radiator cover to any radiators in the area. Radiators are seldom attractive, so a boxed radiator cover, finished to blend with your own decoration, will make the radiator blend in with the area, streamlining the look of the room and creating a useful small shelf above.

Adding small feature shelves above eye-level, such as above a door for example, will also offer extra surfaces for displaying treasures, such as pretty plates, and adding interest to an otherwise dull area.

Creating more space

If after assessing the potential of your hallway you still feel that it is impractically small,

consider whether the space could be put to better use, but also think about the kind of impression you are trying to create. If you feel more comfortable in cosy, intimate rooms or if you prefer to maintain the traditional character of your home, you will need to rely on your flair as a decorator and careful planner to create an impression of space in the hallway. If not, imagine how the downstairs of your house would look if the one of the walls in the hall area were removed to create a larger, open-plan space. The main points against doing this are:

■ The lack of privacy: all visitors and anyone going up or downstairs will enter and pass through your living room.

■ Heating: the hallway serves to protect the rest of the home from draughts, and its removal will open your living room to the elements.

■ Dirt: the hall is a convenient place to leave dirty or wet clothes and shoes, and the floor can be covered accordingly. If the room is open-plan your choice of floor covering will need careful consideration.

These are the negative aspects to consider. On the positive side, you would gain a sense of space and extra light, and you could always maintain a half-height wall where the original dividing wall stood in order to gain the same benefits of the open space while maintaining a visual and practical barrier between the 'hallway' and the living room. Discuss your plans with a professional architect or builder.

A less drastic and more easily achievable alternative is to look at the existing door arrangement and see if it could be slightly altered to make a more usable and practical hall or landing space and extra space in the room beyond, as well. It is possible that some of the doors that open into the hall could be rehung so that they opened in the opposite

Do you have a radiator that could be treated with a cover to provide not only a smarter finish to your hallway or landing but also a narrow ledge for displaying flowers or family photographs? Hanging a mirror in a passageway will further help to increase the sense of depth and will look particularly attractive with lamps in front of it.

Open your imagination and feel free to cross the usual boundaries of what each area of your home is used for. There is no reason a hallway cannot also be used as a dining area. If the space is limited you could bring chairs from around the home to the dining table when they are needed and remove them when they are not.

direction, and this would make the hall or landing area less of an obstacle course. Again, if any rooms lead into each other, it may be that you do not need to have a working door from one of the rooms into the hall and that this could be blocked off, in a temporary or more permanent fashion, and covered with, say, bookshelves, a desk or any other feature you are especially anxious to include in your scheme.

A change of function

If your whole living area is on the small side, yet you have been blessed with what seems to be an incongruously spacious white elephant of a hallway, be thankful. You have the space and opportunity to adapt your hall area into

more practical living space and even to create what you may feel you are lacking elsewhere. If your home lacks a dining room, for instance, the hall could be just the place. If you are desperate for a study, the end of a corridor could fit the bill. And if an extra toilet or shower room is what you need, with the help of the professionals, the understairs cupboard can easily be converted. All you need is imagination, not a lot of space.

Hall/dining area

Formal dining rooms do not play as regular a part in our lives as they once did, so it has become more practical in the small home to make the dining area into a transient feature. With the help of folding chairs and tables, a dining 'room' can be created in a matter of minutes and, as it's unlikely that you will have a constant flow of unexpected visitors in the evening, the hall could be the perfect spot! Look out for drop-leaf or round tables that could stand against a wall by day and be moved to centre stage at night. Folding chairs could be stored under the stairs or brought in from other rooms, or you could create a narrow bench seat along one wall or look out for an old-fashioned settle or even a church pew. When it is covered with an elegant dining cloth and decorated with a candelabra and your finest china and cutlery, the table and its setting will match that of the most intimate restaurants!

Hall/library

Most books require little depth of shelving, which makes the hallway or landing the perfect spot to house them. To create a useful library area, plan your shelving to run around and between doors and even over them and keep a step or stool to hand so that you can get to the top shelf easily. If you can block off one end of the hall and add a chair and adequate lighting, the space could become quite a pleasant retreat!

Hall/telephone room

The hall is a good place to site a phone so that conversations do not interfere with the activities in any of the main rooms, and if you decide to keep the hall an unwelcoming place, it should save on your phone bills! Ideally, there should be a seat of some kind and somewhere to keep directories and write messages. A small side-table or slim chest of drawers and a chair by the telephone socket will do. Fold-down shelf tables are not suitable, however, because the last thing you want to do is struggle with a folding table top with the phone tucked under your chin! If you have only one phone in the home and would like it to be more accessible, you could

The possibilities of a stairwell are often overlooked. It can, of course, be hung attractively with pictures, but you could also put it to more practical use and add shelving for books. Most books require only a slim shelf, so a library of this kind will not restrict access through the passageway.

Console tables are ideal for landings and hallways and, combined with a chair, make the business of taking phone calls far more comfortable. If an easy chair is not a practical option in the space you have available, a small stool or fold-down bench could do the job for you.

Hallways and understairs areas are notoriously awkward, but with the right treatment, they can become attractive as well as practical places. A small-scale desk offers a useful study or writing area and has been combined with an open-backed chair so it doesn't appear to take up as much room. To make such a small space even more practical, you could investigate various shelving systems, which usually include pull-out desks and a range of storage options.

consider knocking through a small arch or window between the hallway and an adjacent room and siting the telephone on the ledge, so that calls can be taken on either side. As well as making an interesting feature, you also have the bonus of allowing more light into the hall from the adjoining room.

Hall/study

Although a hallway or landing may not be the retreat favoured by budding authors or be an appropriate place for serious revision, if you need a desk area for nothing more than keeping household accounts or writing an occasional letter, it could be just the place. If there is room, a desk and chair could be introduced, but if space is limited, consider a fold-down shelf attached to the wall and a basic stool below. Shelves to either side can be used to house papers and books, and you could always add a folding screen if you want to provide extra privacy.

The understairs cupboard

If you are after something a little more secluded, consider your understairs storage space. Left as a simple cupboard, this area inevitably becomes filled with household junk, but cleared out and fitted with shelves, a desk and decent lighting, it could soon be something far more useful. By removing the permanent door and replacing it with a curtain you will give yourself enough room to sit comfortably, yet will be able to shut it off from view whenever it is not in use.

The understairs cupboard is one of the most useful areas in your hallway, so do not discount it too quickly. Although the storage space is undoubtedly useful, it may suit your own requirements better to make alternative use of the space it occupies. With the right treatment this tiny place could become anything from a kitchen area, a washing machine space – even a spot for an extra bed! Talk to an interior designer or architect if inspiration fails you.

If your kitchen isn't large enough for all your needs, why not extend into the hallway? If it is decorated in a sympathetic way to complement the surrounding living space, the understairs area could offer a smart solution to your shortage of workspace or storage. If your home is an open plan apartment take a look at the small-scale kitchen appliances now available – you may find you could fit all you need into a small understairs area.

If your hallway or landing is rather gloomy, look at ways of allowing extra light through. Perhaps you could add glazed panels to internal doors so that the hallway can benefit from the light in connecting rooms, and you may be able to adapt some doors so that they can be held open at all times.

Lighting

When it comes to planning the lighting in areas such as the hall, landing and other corridors in the home, your main priority must be safety; the second consideration is to add interest and make the area more visually appealing.

If there are small children or elderly people in your home, safety will obviously be more of an issue, but in any home it is important to make sure that potentially dark or gloomy areas are well lit during the day and at night, so that people do not trip on the stairs or fumble in corridors. For this you need a good combination of natural and task lighting.

Natural light

It is likely that there will be little or even no natural daylight entering your hallway and landing so, unless you are happy to rely on electric lighting twenty-four hours a day, take a look at how you might allow yourself to benefit more from a supply that is, after all, free as well as more appealing! Could your front and any internal doors be replaced with a design that allows the light to filter through? You needn't sacrifice privacy in favour of light if you opt for a style that perhaps incorporates stained, etched or frosted glass. A slightly more drastic, but very effective option, is to knock through an external wall in the hall and stair area to create a window space. Again the glass you choose to fit could be etched or stained if you are overlooked, but you will gain substantially from it as a light source.

Artificial light

To check that your current lighting is adequate – although you will probably be only too well aware if it isn't – note how your stairs are illuminated in both artificial and natural light. Ideally, you should be able to see the stair treads clearly, while the riser remains in shadow so that it is perfectly clear where to

Lighting the hall

Effective hallway lighting needs to be bright and well directed:

□ Low-wattage bulbs will produce a rather gloomy light, so opt for fittings and shades that can take 100 watts in order to keep the area looking bright and to make it safer. If you wish, you can keep some areas more softly lit, but combine table lamps or soft uplighters with a stronger beam, directed where it is needed, such as towards the stairs.

□ Adjustable spot-lights mounted on the wall or ceiling are useful because you can experiment with the angle until you get exactly the right degree of illumination on the treads and risers.

□ Wall bracket lights with standard shades tend to be rather ineffective as they cast the light only up and down the walls and not over the lanes of traffic. In addition, in a small, narrow hallway, illuminating the sides of the corridor, however dimly, will focus attention on them and accentuate the narrowness of the area.

□ Don't forget that lighting can be used to create interest as well as a safe area – and a hallway more than any other room needs to be livened up and given some drama. Highlight collections, such as pictures or plates displayed on the walls, by using spot-lights, picture lights or uplighters, but avoid freestanding floor lamps, which are too much of a hazard in a confined area.

place each foot as you go up and down the stairs. This requires a good light source from above, but also means that any light source in the hall below does not interfere with the balance by illuminating the risers of the stairs. Also make sure that any fitted electric lights don't glare into your eyes as you use the stairs.

Decorating a small hall

A hallway should be a welcoming place – somewhere that reflects the style of your home and makes an instant impact. However it also needs to be decorated practically, because it is going to suffer more wear and tear than any other room in the home and, however small it is, it won't be long before scuffs and stains diminish its appeal.

Colours

First, decide on the colour scheme. Turn to Chapter 2 on colour if you still lack confidence in choosing colours. It helps to link the feel of a small home and to create more of a general impression of space if the hallway is decorated in a way that blends with the schemes in each of the rooms it opens on to. Remember that doors will often be left open and you don't want a hallway to clash with every other room, so aim to create a sense of harmony as you stand in the hall. Don't let that scare you into playing safe, however, so that you either decorate every room in the same colours or stick to a dull, neutral shade for the hall. You will probably find that a certain palette of colours naturally appeals to you and that you tend to use them more than any others. If so, you should find it fairly easy to select one that complements all of your schemes. Yellow, for example, is not only a warm welcoming colour, which is perfect for a hallway, but it also works well with blues, greens and oranges and, depending on the shade of yellow you choose, with other colours, too. Adding a small dash of yellow to your blue living room or green kitchen will make an instant link with the hallway beyond.

It is worth remembering that, as you spend relatively little time in your hallway, you can afford to be rather more daring than you might normally be. Why not go for a bold gold when you would normally opt for daffodil yellow or for rose pink when you would normally settle for a more subtle sorbet. Because halls are often cold, draughty places, a warm colour will make it feel more cosy and look better in subdued light than a pastel, cream or white, and blues, greens and violets will appear too cold.

Break it up

If you still feel rather daunted at the thought of covering a whole wall in something quite daring, consider incorporating a dado rail into your scheme. These not only allow you to combine a bright shade with something less dramatic, but they are also ideal for adding interest to a dull corridor, with the additional advantage of allowing you to use a more practical wall covering along the lower level of the room where hall walls suffer most. Traditionally, a dado rail was a wooden moulding that, sited at approximately the height of an average chair back, protected the wall from scuffs and knocks. Today you do not need to add a wooden moulding to create the decorative effect you are after. You could put up a toning wallpaper border at dado-height or paint a dado-height line along the length of the room, using masking tape and a spirit level to guide you.

Be aware that anything on the walls that is picked out in a bold colour will bring attention to the sides of the room and emphasize the narrowness of a tight corridor. You can use the opposite rule to your benefit, however, and 'lose' the impression of narrowness, along with any unattractive features, by painting such things as radiators and skirting boards in the same colour as the walls so that they blend in with the background and don't jar the eye.

You can create an impression of space by continuing a similar colour scheme throughout a small home, but if that option doesn't appeal to you, at least consider how the colour scheme of a hall or landing will work with the rooms that lead off it. The neutral yet warm shades of terracotta and wood in this hallway are unlikely to clash with any other scheme it meets.

Material matters

Once you've decided on your colour scheme, think practically about the materials. In a small hallway, a hard-wearing paint or wallpaper is the best choice, for practicality, but also because eggshell or gloss paint and vinyl wallpaper have more of a sheen than flat emulsion and this helps to reflect any available light around the room.

Illusions of space

If you choose the right colours and patterns you are already doing as much as you can to ensure your small hallway is decorated to best effect, but you still have one more powerful tool to use in the fight against space and light restrictions – a mirror. Large mirrors are wonderfully effective at reflecting light and increasing the impression of space in any area, so it is worth investing in something rather grand for your hallway or the landing. Hang one opposite a doorway or a window and it will create the impression of greater depth in the corridor and reflect light back into the hall. If that option is not open to you, at least hang the mirror where there is something of interest on the opposite wall. A long mirror running along the corridor above dado-height will maximize the effect.

Accessories

A hallway needs to be given as much interest as possible – however small it may be – so look for pieces and collections that can be attractively displayed to brighten it up. In a small space this means making the most of any wall space that is available. Don't discount the space between door frames, and even above doors, as potential display areas. Small pictures, perhaps united by a traditional display ribbon, can be hung in the narrowest of areas, while plates, dolls or masks make eye-catching features above a doorframe or hung up the stairwell.

In a small space, particularly, it is more

ergonomic if the pieces used to decorate and add interest to the area also have some practical value, so look for ways of brightening up some of your more boring necessities –such as an umbrella stand, a mirror frame or a lampshade – to display them to full effect. If you are looking out for accessories, choose the ones that offer extra storage space or perhaps a spare hook for keys.

Flooring

All hallways need practical flooring running from the front door in order to minimize the amount of dirt brought indoors and to look good as long as possible. If you prefer something softer underfoot than practical tiling, vinyl or wood, at least make sure that you have the largest doormat you can find (ideally one that is recessed into your flooring so that it can be vacuumed and doesn't restrict the movement of the front door) and try to choose a carpeting with stain-resistant qualities and a high content of man-made fibres so that it maintains its looks for as long as possible. Another option to consider is carpet

Fixing mirrored glass above dado height helps to give a dark and narrow passageway extra life and an impression of greater depth. Try to provide something of interest on the opposite wall so that the mirror can reflect something other than a bare wall.

tiles, because you can easily replace any that become too worn or stained.

To increase the impression of space, you should aim for wall-to-wall continuity rather than breaking up the area with too many rugs or different types of floor covering, and keep to plain designs or very small patterns. If you have opted for a practical, hard-wearing flooring in your living room (as is advisable), consider extending it into your hallway and up the stairs to give the greatest impression of continuity. In fact, using the same carpeting in as many rooms as possible is ideal in the small home.

Window treatments

These should be kept simple to allow as much light as possible into the area, so go for blinds, shutters or no curtaining at all. Long or full curtains are not practical in an area that sees so much traffic, the only exception being in front of the front door, where a long, lined curtain covering the door and its frame will help to keep out draughts. Ideally, such curtains should be hung from a special pole that opens with the door or from a pole that is wide enough to pull the curtain right out of the way when it is not in use.

Spindles, rather than a solid stair surround, allow the eye to pass through and form an impression of open space, and the simple blind at the window permits maximum light to enter. Practical flooring is a must in any hallway – whatever its size – and durable tiling is ideal.

9 Children's rooms

This is somewhere you can have real fun! Children's bedrooms are where you can let your imagination and use of colour have full rein – and you should do so, whatever the size of the space. Bedrooms are special places for children, somewhere they can call their own, store their personal treasures and become lost in their own fantasy worlds. If you can create somewhere that will inspire their imaginations, look good and be comfortable as well as practical, you can be sure that, no matter how small the room, your children will have fond memories of it long after the wallpaper has been stripped off the walls and you have all moved on.

Allocating space

When you have to decide who will sleep where, most parents tend to take the largest room for themselves and allocate the box room as the nursery. This is not always the best distribution of your available space, however. True, a baby does not need a lot in the way of sleeping room, but that baby will quickly grow into a toddler, whose toys will be large and bulky, and into a schoolchild, who will need a desk, somewhere to entertain friends and so on. A child's bedroom is far more than somewhere to sleep, it is the centre of all their activities. An adult requires space to store clothes, sleep and dress; a child also needs room to play, rest and (later) work, as well as somewhere to keep toys and games. Essentially, a child needs room to grow. Not only that, if you are just starting a family, it is more than likely that before long another baby may have to share a bedroom with a sibling or two. So, unless you are happy to face a change around in a couple of years' time and to start your decorating from scratch once again – or are lucky enough to have a playroom elsewhere in the home – it may be prudent to give yourself the smaller room and allocate the precious space to your children.

If, however, that is not possible or if even the largest of your bedrooms is on the small side, you may have to look at ways of opening up another area of your home for your children to use in addition to their bedroom, either as somewhere to store toys or to use as a centre for their activities, such as painting, doing puzzles or creating something out of nothing. If you have stairs, that versatile understairs cupboard could be transformed into a den where no adult is allowed; a corner of a large hallway could house a small table and chairs or a large armoire for storing toys; an alcove in a family room could be fitted with a fold-down table and used to display your child's works of art; a guest room could double as a playroom; or a window seat could be built in a large window downstairs with a lift-up lid in which to store toys and painting equipment. Young children like to be wherever you are, so a play area is

A baby's room needs to offer little more than somewhere to sleep and store clothes and equipment, but if you are redesigning the room now, it is still worth looking at built-in wardrobes. Fitted designs offer flexible storage space, which can be adapted as your baby grows and has different requirements – and it will ensure that you make the most of the space available.

always useful for allowing you to get on with whatever you want while they play nearby.

Changing and developing

Whatever size of room you are going to re-design and decorate, the most important thing to remember is that the demands placed upon it are going to change more rapidly than in any other room. The first five years of your child's life alone will be a series of swift developments, and it won't seem long before a babe in arms is starting school. So, unless you are the sort of person who relishes the opportunity to get out the paint-brush and fabric samples every twelve months, the fabrics and wallpapers you choose now will have to undergo several subtle facelifts in order to keep your developing offspring both happy and comfortable, and

any furniture, lighting, storage and electric socket arrangements will need to be enormously flexible. The preparation and planning stage you undertake now will be crucial, so think carefully before you make any decisions and, in addition to considering the suggestions in this chapter and in Chapter 1, talk to friends with older children about how they have had to adapt their homes over the years.

Nursery basics

You need very little space for a small baby – especially for the first six months or so – and, as many parents prefer to keep their babies in their own bedroom for the first twelve weeks, you may find it just as easy to keep everything else you need in there, too. All the items you need to incorporate in your baby's room are covered below.

Somewhere to sleep

A large Moses basket and a stand for it may be a worthwhile investment in order to postpone by about three months the time you have to take up extra floor space with a bulky cot. A Moses basket can be carried around the home with you during the day and brought into your room and placed on the stand (which is collapsible) at night.

If you live in a ground-floor flat or don't mind carrying a heavy carrycot and pram frame up and downstairs, a pram is a perfectly adequate place for your baby to sleep, and is likely to be used out and about during the day.

Swinging cribs are not very portable and will not last long, but they are pretty and don't take up as much space by your bedside as a standard cot. If the baby is going to be in your room for the first three months, a crib may be worth considering.

Check the amount of floor space you have available before you buy a cot, because they vary quite substantially in size, with cot beds being especially variable. If the cot has to be positioned with one side up against a wall, but it has a useful storage box underneath or a drop-side mechanism, make sure that these features are accessible from the side you envisaged. Cot beds save space in the future, but only if you do not envisage having another baby until after your first child has moved out of it, which will be at about three years plus.

When you are allocating rooms, do not assume that the smallest should naturally be the baby's. Children spend a lot of time in their bedrooms as they grow up and accumulate a lot of bulky toys so consider handing over a larger room to your youngsters. Giving them more space will make it easier to avoid hazards, such as having the bed next to a window. Always bear in mind the safety points listed on page 141 when planning children's rooms.

Two sharing

In a small home it is more than likely that, at some stage, you will have two children sharing a bedroom. This can work well, offering extra company and security, but as time goes by it will become even more important that each child has his or her own space, not just to sleep, but to store toys and play. The plan will depend on the ages of the children, but consider some of the following to help make the plan successful:

☐ A screen makes a useful room divider, giving both children privacy. Look at ways of creating a divide with a piece of furniture, or with a purpose-built screen. This could be covered with fabric, designed as a pin board or even painted with blackboard paint to make a chalk board. To make the screen work hard, add hooks for hanging bags or dressing up clothes.

☐ If you have bunk beds for two children, can they be put in the middle of the room, as a visual divide, so that each child has one half of the room space?

☐ Small toys, which can be a hazard to under-threes, can be kept in higher wall-mounted boxes, so that older children can reach them but babies cannot.

☐ Give both children separate bedside lights so that one can read while the other sleeps.

☐ Buy one wardrobe with two hanging rails, one high and one low, and allocate a separate rail to each child. Or use the alcoves at the sides of a chimney breast to create two sets of hanging space. The rails can be hung at appropriate heights for each child and shelves fitted above. Hang curtains across the alcoves to conceal any clutter.

A chest of drawers/changing unit

You will need somewhere to store clothes and nappy-changing equipment. At this stage of life, babies don't need wardrobes because their clothes are small enough to be folded and kept in drawers.

Look out for a design that is about hip height, as it can be topped with a changing mat and used as a changing table, too, which will save both the space and money that a dedicated changing table will require. When you are changing your baby you will need to be extremely vigilant and not turn your back for an instant, so that he or she doesn't roll off. (To make you feel more secure, you could make a high-sided tray which could sit on top of the chest and be attached to the wall.) The top drawer can be used as a storage compartment for nappy-changing equipment, such as lotions, creams and cotton wool, and the rest of the drawer space can be used for clothes. Buying a traditional-looking chest for this purpose, such as a chunky pine design, will also allow the same piece of furniture to be used for different storage purposes for years to come.

An alternative arrangement for nappy changing is to invest now in a worktop or desk-style unit that will offer adequate space for a changing mat (bearing in mind the safety points mentioned above) and will last for many years as a play area and, later, perhaps a school desk.

Do not feel pressurized into buying a special changing unit, especially if you are short of space. Osteopaths recommend that the best place to change your baby is on your bed, with you kneeling at the side, although you may have to change the bedcover more often than normal!

Few families have the space to allow children the luxury of a bedroom each, but this cleverly designed work station is ideal for sharing siblings. The older child has room for a computer while the younger has space to read and draw. The shelves between not only provide a natural division but are a way of incorporating storage without using valuable wall space.

Somewhere to store nappies

Pretty nappy stackers are more of a luxury than a space-saving device, because you can rarely fit a whole pack of nappies into a stacker at once and so have to store the rest of the packet somewhere else anyway. Storing a packet of nappies or washable nappies and accessories in the chest of drawers on which you will be changing the baby is a more practicable solution, but they can just as well be kept at the bottom of a wardrobe or under the bed.

A chair for feeding

If the baby is in your room, it is likely that you will do the night feeds in bed. If the baby is in a nursery, however, you will need somewhere comfortable to sit while you nurse. A small armchair is ideal, but choose one with washable slip covers if possible, because it is sure to need cleaning regularly.

For pre-schoolers

Pre-school children spend a lot of time in their bedrooms, although they will also want to play wherever you are too. At this age the bedroom needs to be at its most practical and yet to offer the most scope for creating a fantasy world within its four walls. In addition to (or to replace) the nursery basics, you will need at least the following:

Somewhere to sleep

When space is short it is worth keeping your toddler in a cot or cot bed for as long as possible because it takes up much less floor space than a single bed. When you do come to buy a bed, look for designs with underbed storage that is easy for children to use.

Antique-style sleigh beds and box beds make good starter beds. Not only are they attractive, but they have high sides to keep

your children secure. Buying a child-size bed is probably not worthwhile, however, because the time will inevitably arrive when a full-size single bed is needed, and a child-size bed cannot be put to use in a guest room or elsewhere.

A bunk bed may already be worth considering. Although your own child will still be too young to sleep on the top bunk, in a couple of years' time, when he or she is five or six, it will be safe and offer the opportunity for friends to stay in a small room and, when the time comes, be available for a second child. In the meantime you can always use the top bunk for extra storage space, but remember to remove the ladder until you want your child to use it. Some designs of bunk bed allow you to stand the two beds separately or on top of each other, so you can

keep one of the beds in a spare room until you feel that it is time to add it on or use it in the spare room again after the need for bunks has passed.

When you buy any design of bunk bed, check that the mattresses provided are adequate and that there is enough room for a child to sit up in the lower bunk and for you to perch there for story time.

A table and chairs

All toddlers need somewhere to paint and draw and to play with construction toys or modelling clay, so a child-size table and two chairs are essential and don't take up very much room. There is little point in looking for space-saving folding designs because children like to set up the table and chairs themselves and will

Admittedly this room is not small, but it contains plenty of ideas on how to provide children with good storage and work spaces. A blackboard area will save the paintwork, and a pin-board will protect the walls. Taking the shelving up to the ceiling creates ample storage space, but remember not to put a tantalizing collection of toys on the higher shelves – it is asking for accidents to happen as children struggle to reach them.

inevitably trap their fingers in anything not designed specifically for children.

Make the most of a spare alcove or a bay window, and fit a permanent work surface in there, but remember that if you construct something at toddler level, it will not be long before it is outgrown.

If drawing is your child's passion, make the most of your wall space by fixing hardboard along the bottom part of one or two walls and painting them with blackboard paint to create a permanent chalkboard area. An appropriately wide dado rail could be used as a narrow shelf for chalks. You could cover another part of wall space with pinboard material to provide gallery space for your children's works of art, without damaging the wallpaper.

Bookshelves

Books play an important part in the development of pre-school children, so allow plenty of room for a collection to grow. You could allocate an alcove to fit with shelves (starting low down at toddler level) and use the out-of-reach shelves for displaying bits and pieces not in permanent use or storing out-of-season clothes in smart boxes or suitcases.

If you have enough floor space, create a reading area by placing two small book shelves at right angles in a corner of the room and covering the floor within with cushions or bean-bags to make it cosy. You could paint the backs of the bookshelves with blackboard paint to make them more useful, and attractive.

If space is more limited and one end of the

Small, awkward corners make a room all the more appealing to children and can often be used more effectively than they would be in an adult room. There is just enough room here for a little desk area and book shelving for a girl. Notice how, although this is obviously a little girl's room, it has been decorated in a fashion that would appeal equally to more adult tastes, making it longer lasting and adaptable for the future.

Adapt your shelving designs to suit the scale of the room. In a small room this cubed layout looks the part and is perfect for children. A low hanging rail for clothes enables a pre-school child to dress him- or herself and is flexible enough to be useful in the future.

bed is against a wall, book shelves can be positioned there, too, allowing your child easy access to reading matter once he or she is in bed at night and, during the day, by climbing onto the bed. Be careful not to fix shelves where they could be a hazard to a toddler bouncing on a bed and remember that the furniture is likely to be moved around at least once, so don't make the position of any shelving too restrictive.

Floor space to play and pretend

Free floor space is essential for giving your child room to lay out tea parties, set up train sets and so on. Imaginary play is at its peak at this stage and it helps if there is space to indulge it. Toys are generally large at this time, too, so bear in mind that any spare corners may soon be filled by miniature plastic kitchens or work-stations, dolls' houses and so on.

It is wonderful if you also have a spare alcove in which to create miniature shops, hairdressing shop, puppet theatres and so on, but do not feel that you are depriving your child if that is unachievable. Children can create games from the simplest of objects, and an old suitcase filled with dressing-up clothes and kept under the bed offers just as much scope for play.

A wardrobe

Once your child is walking, wardrobe space becomes more of an issue, although for many years a small gentleman's wardrobe (or tall-boy) or a child's wardrobe will suffice and save on floor space. Look for designs that have a high and low rail to offer most hanging space. This allows you to hang up the clothes you want your child to be able to reach, while keeping out-of-season clothes out of the way. If you don't buy a wardrobe designed with children in mind, try not to choose one that closes too sharply and may

trap fingers. See Storage space (pages 144–45) for more wardrobe options.

If you don't have room for a wardrobe you could fix a row of Shaker-style peg hooks along the wall, perhaps at dado-height, and hang clothes on stylish hangers. At this stage, children's clothes look attractive enough in their own right to allow this. It will also help to encourage children to hang up their own clothes if the pegs are at a height they can reach themselves. Underwear and shoes can be kept in drawstring bags (with very short strings) hung from the same pegs to release drawer space too.

Safety

Whatever the size of your child's bedroom, it is vital that it is designed with safety in mind. In a small room it is especially easy to create unintentional hazards, simply because you are trying to do too much with a confined space and a child may have less free floor space to play in. Check for the following in your room plan:

☐ All the furniture you choose should have rounded edges or should be fitted with plastic safety corners.

☐ Fit locks or even bars to windows so that they cannot be opened without an adult's supervision.

☐ Screw free-standing furniture to the walls so that it cannot be pulled over.

☐ Cover radiators with a decorative cover or guard them while babies are tiny and crawling.

☐ Keep furniture and beds away from windows and cover windows in safety glass.

☐ Avoid lamps with trailing flexes that could be tripped over.

Older children

It doesn't take long for children to develop their individual personalities and have their own ideas about how their bedroom should look. If you include them in the planning for their bedroom they will be much happier – and it will save you having to tear down what you've done and start again. This section is aimed primarily in the five to eleven age range. Teenagers require something more akin to a bedsit, so turn to Chapter 4 on bedrooms for further ideas.

Once children start school they may be at home during less of the day, but they will have a new set of needs for their bedroom – and of course, the demand for more storage space continues to grow and grow. Now is the time to consider the following points:

Beds and platforms

When a room is small, it is worth looking at ways of increasing the available floor area by being a bit more imaginative with your use of the space available. The bed is usually the largest single item in the room and, although it may currently serve to hide a multitude of clutter beneath it, it is more practical to look at raising it off the ground to create more useful storage space or a work area below. Children are likely to welcome the idea too for its novelty value and because they love the idea of retreating up a ladder to their own 'den'.

If you are sufficiently skilled, it is possible to create a platform for a mattress (it will need to be very strong) and to build in either large drawer space or simple clothes hanging space, covered by a blind or curtain. You will need to have a guard running along the edge of the platform and a firmly fixed ladder attached to one end too, but once you have established the basic framework you can use your imagination to make the area into anything from a pirate ship or car to a fairy tale castle or pink grotto, using paint, fabric and shaped pieces of MDF.

If you are not so handy with woodworking tools, don't despair. There are plenty of ready-made alternatives, and several companies create custom-made platform beds to fit into the most awkward of spaces. Most useful at this age is a bed and work area combination. Usually made from pine, these units generally consist of a bed area above (with a ladder for access), and a desk, chair and storage space below.

A work surface/desk

When the room is small, it is also worth looking at ways of incorporating a desk into a run of fitted storage units (see Built-in furniture, page 145) or having one built into an alcove. If you are planning to stay in the home a long time, the room may eventually become a study or a guest room, in which case the area will still be useful as a dressing-table. A girl may want the desk area to double as a dressing-table at this stage, in which case provide plenty of drawer space, plus shelves above and around it to store both study items and trinkets. A mirror can easily be fixed to the wall above.

Whatever sort of desk you opt for, be it free-standing or fitted, it will probably need to be large enough to cope with a television, hi-fi or a computer, and remember that there should be enough electric sockets nearby for these and for extra lighting.

Room for guests

Children love to have friends staying the night, but rather than trying to include an extra bed in your plan, look at space-saving bed ideas, such as armchairs that fold out to a single mattress, sofa beds (if you can afford the room they take up), blow-up mattresses or folding Z-beds, which can be stored flat when not in use.

If your floor area is limited, make the most of high ceilings by adding a raised sleeping area. Perfect for older children, this kind of structure has all the excitement of a 'den' while releasing floor space for work and storage.

Positioning furniture

When it comes to juggling the pieces you have to incorporate on your piece of squared paper, remember that the scheme will have to be flexible and adapt over the years. Think ahead as much as you can, but also bear in mind the following points:

■ Beds should not be next to a window as children will inevitably bounce on them and there may be an accident.

■ Don't put a cot next to a radiator because babies could burn themselves if they put an arm or a leg through the bars.

■ Toys or games shouldn't be positioned on shelves so high that children need to climb to get them – they could fall.

■ You will need enough room next to a cot or bed to help babies in and out and for you to sit to read stories.

■ Even toddlers will need some room for a bedside-table for books, tissues, a night light and maybe a child's clock.

Storage space

The type of storage facilities you incorporate into a child's bedroom should, like everything else in the room, be practical, flexible and safe for small hands. The type of system you opt for will finally depend on your budget, how long you will be staying in the home and how many children will be using the room. Basically you need to choose between free-standing furniture, fitted furniture and modular systems or a combination of all three.

Free-standing furniture

The greatest flexibility is provided by free-standing furniture and storage units, which allow you to alter the layout as your child grows up and if another child later moves into the room. It is less expensive usually than fitted furniture, and it can be added to as and when you need more pieces. However, it will never offer such efficient use of the available space in a small room as built-in furniture can, and should be bolted to the walls in order to make it completely safe.

When space is tight, it helps to keep your design simple and to provide plenty of wardrobe space in which to clear away any clutter. This design offers an older child a greater feeling of independence than traditional bunks would provide, and the wall space lost by positioning the two beds in this way, is reclaimed in the form of fitted units below the bunk.

Built-in furniture

Built-in furniture makes the most of every inch of space, from floor to ceiling, and also creates a unified, integrated finish, which is flattering to the small bedroom. The most awkwardly shaped of bedrooms can be made more efficient with the help of well-designed fitted furniture, and you should be able to buy units that offer internal flexibility, such as a choice of heights for the hanging rail and the divisions of the shelf space, as well as features such as sliding doors to maintain the available floor space.

Choose a plain, hard-wearing finish for the doors. You can always add extra decoration to them yourselves in the form of stencils, stickers or even a mural, repainting them or replacing them as your child grows up.

If you are considering installing built-in furniture it is vital that you plan ahead and include any features that will be necessary in years to come.

Modular or system furniture

This type of furniture offers you the opportunity to increase your storage space as you need it by adding on more units. Although the furniture has a semi-fitted look it is ready-made and requires self-assembly, so it may not help you to make the most of awkward corners in the same way as a built in, custom-made cupboard may.

Decorating children's rooms

The decorative finishes you use in a child's room should be stimulating and cheerful, but above all hard-wearing. Paint is most practical as it is easy to touch up if necessary and, if you choose an oil-based paint, such as eggshell or gloss, it is easy to keep clean. If you prefer to work with emulsion, choose vinyl silk rather than matt paint to give a wipe-clean surface. Vinyl wallpaper is another option, although it is more expensive and you must be prepared for it to get splashed with paint sometimes or

nicked accidentally. A good compromise is to have a hard-wearing paint below dado-height, a pretty paper above, where it is in less danger from grubby hands.

To keep your room space adaptable, avoid going overboard on babyish and too obviously boyish or feminine decorations. If the room is small and dark, a warm colour such as a sunny yellow is ideal as it will be appropriate for any sex. Light, south- or west-facing small rooms could be painted a fresh light violet or green, combined with white, to increase the impression of space. You can

Don't rush to take out traditional features in order to create a more spacious look. A small room with a chimney breast is not only pretty, it offers more useful space than you might think. Alcoves are perfect places for incorporating storage units, even if they are quite shallow. The units in this shallow recess have been brought forwards of the breast by a few inches but without destroying the original look.

Converting basement or roof space or even playing around with the original structure of the home is often the only way of creating the space we need, but it does mean that we have to cope with awkward features, such as a staircase intruding into a bedroom or limited space for a sleeping area. The traditional spindles keep the staircase area looking open and spacious, while a built-in bed offers the opportunity for more cupboard and shelf space around the window. Even on a ground floor, it is vital to fit safety locks to windows to prevent children being able to open them on their own. If at all possible, avoid positioning beds next to windows.

always add particularly boyish or girlish touches in the form of accessories.

Let your child get involved with the decorating and choice of furnishings, but restrict themed or age-related furnishings to the items that are cheap and easy to replace, such as duvet covers, roller blinds and lampshades. It won't be long before the next craze arrives and there will be demands for a revamped bedroom! If the basics, such as the upholstery, flooring and main curtaining are more adult designs, the room will be easier to adapt as years go by, and it will be more easily converted into a guest room if necessary.

Window dressings

If you have generously handed over the master bedroom to your children, it is likely that they now have the largest and most impressive windows in the home. Nevertheless, you should still resist the urge to dress them elaborately. Floor-length curtains are like magnets to toddlers who, as soon as your back is turned, will have tried swinging from them, pulling themselves up on them or, at least, covered the fabric with sticky finger marks. Instead, your main priorities should be practicality and light resistance, so that you have at least a slim chance of a lie-in in

Toy storage

A child's possessions seem to increase at an alarming rate, so whatever type of furniture you have chosen, you may also have to consider some of the following storage options. Remember to make storage easy to access and as appealing as possible to encourage youngsters to tidy up after themselves.

☐ Plastic crates and wicker baskets, which can be kept under the bed, at the bottom of a wardrobe or in a corner, are ideal for quick tidy-ups. Crates have the advantage of being stackable, and you can label them (with pictures as well as words) so that certain types of toy are kept together.

☐ Adjustable shelving, created by fixing shelves onto adjustable shelving brackets, can increase the amount of shelving space, and also enable you to play around with its height, giving you the flexibility to move it as your child grows up or as furniture of varying heights is placed in front of it. Always screw the shelves into the brackets to make them extra safe and secure.

☐ When you are choosing a bed, consider a divan with fitted drawers or opt for a model with a free-standing drawer on castors. Alternatively, smart boxes and suitcases can be used to keep toys stored neatly under the bed.

☐ Make the most of nooks and crannies. Every corner offers storage potential, and even a redundant fireplace can be used to store a dolls' house or other treasures, while a hammock can be suspended from the ceiling to store a large collection of cuddly toys.

☐ Hooks or pegs fixed at dado-height allow you to hang a collection of draw-string bags or fabric pockets. which can be used to store small toys and odds and ends.

☐ Window seats with a hollow box and lift-up lids make the most of often under-used space in a bay window or an alcove. Ideally, the design should be one with a gap between the lid and the front of the seat, so that small fingers don't get trapped if the lid falls down.

the morning. Both curtains and blinds can be lined with black-out fabric, or you could combine lighter, more washable curtains with a cheap blind, to create a double barrier against light and draughts. Keep to simple curtain headings; you can always dress up the curtain pole with fancy finials or add a shaped pelmet for a more decorative touch.

Lighting

Your child's bedroom will be used for a wider range of activities than an adult's bedroom, so the lighting scheme needs careful planning to meet those needs now and to adapt to future demands.

The nursery

In a nursery avoid central lights with pendent shades as your baby will be lying in a cot looking directly up into the bulb. Instead, look out for large translucent shades that encase the bulb completely or avoid a central ceiling light altogether and opt for wall lights. Uplighters cast the glare from the bulb upwards creating a softer yet equally efficient light. You will need two or three such wall lights in a small to average room.

Dimmer switches are extremely useful for making nocturnal visits without having to turn on a bright, glaring light.

Plug-in night lights do not require a surface

around frequently that could be impractical. A small spot-light directed over the bed area could be the answer, but keep the light itself away from little hands, as it will get very hot. Children's table lamps should be made with a sturdy base, so they cannot be knocked over, a hideaway flex and a covered bulb.

The light switches in a child's bedroom should be positioned low enough for them to be able to turn them on and off themselves or you will find yourself in and out doing the job for them.

Desk lighting may be required for homework or drawing. To avoid using up precious sockets that could be used for computers and so on in the future, consider fitting a track of spot-lights to the ceiling so that one spot-light can be directed over the desk area, while others provide task or decorative lighting effects elsewhere.

If night lights are needed, you might consider recessed downlighters, but if the position of the bed alters, you run the risk of having a bright light shining directly over the pillow once more.

Flooring

For the first few years, a child is going to spend most of the time crawling, sitting and playing on the floor, so the type of finish or covering you give it is particularly important. A small bedroom will undoubtedly appear larger if the same floor finish is extended from wall to wall, be it fitted carpeting or a hard surface, but fitted carpeting may be impracticable and hard surfaces may be uncomfortable, unless they are covered with a cheap, soft, washable rug, so for once it may be better to concentrate less on creating an impression of space and instead to make the best use of the free floor space you have.

Hard surfaces will offer more comfort if covered with a rug, but always ensure that you attach a non-slip backing.

Don't be scared to be bold just because a room is small. A child's bedroom can take bright colours, as long as you bear in mind the effect of warm and cool colours, and the natural light the room receives (see Chapter 2). Vinyl silk paints or even varnish on the walls provides them extra protection from a child's attack and helps to reflect the light around a small room.

to stand on and they do not have trailing flexes. Against these advantages, however, are the facts that they tend to cast a softer light than table-top lights, and you will need to have enough wall space to ensure that the socket area is not covered by furniture.

Toddlers and older children

The nursery basics still apply, but remember that just at the time when trailing flexes are most hazardous, your child will be demanding a bedside light in order to look at books. An ideal solution is to have a light switch or pull cord by the bed so that your child can control the light without having a hot bulb near the bed. If the furniture is going to move

■ Varnished floorboards should be covered with a rug for comfort and sound insulation. There is little point spending a lot of time painting your floorboards with an attractive design if you need to cover them with a rug to make them comfortable to play on. If the boards have wide gaps between them pieces of puzzles and small toys will disappear, so consider filling or moving them first.

■ Coir, sisal or seagrass are hard wearing and durable, but their coarse texture makes them unsuitable for crawlers and for playing on.

■ Cork tiles are cheap, easy to clean and warm underfoot. The tiles are available only in natural colours and they cannot be used with some types of underfloor heating.

■ Carpeting is practicable only if it is a stain-resistant design, but it still will not be as stain resistant as a hard surface. If you are determined to have carpeting don't go for large patterns (in a bid to hide marks) as they will dominate a small room, and remember that a thick pile makes playing with some floor toys more difficult.

■ Carpet tiles offer some of the comfort of carpet, with added practicality. You can replace any that become badly stained or if some areas suffer more wear than others.

■ Cushioned vinyl has the same benefits as cork tiles, but it comes in a wide range of colours and designs. Be careful not to choose a design that looks too clinical.

■ Wooden laminate flooring offers the attractive appearance and durability of bare boards but with greater insulating qualities.

■ Linoleum is not quite as hard-wearing as cushioned vinyl, but it actually contains bactericidal qualities and is resistant to stains, making it ideal for nurseries. You can create wonderful designs using different colours of linoleum, but it needs to be laid by a professional.

If you can wipe it clean it's the perfect floor covering! If you are considering patterned vinyl for a small bedroom, remember to keep it small scale so that it does not dominate the room. If you want to use stripes, they should run between the walls that are closest together (the narrowest dimensions of the room) in order to emphasize the full extent of that width.

10 Putting a scheme together

When you have decided on a theme for a room, the range of colours you can use will become more obvious. You will be able to eliminate some immediately because of the light your room receives or the effect you want to achieve (remember that cool colours such as blues and greens will make the room seem more spacious, whereas warm colours will advance towards you), but experiment with tester pots of other colours to see which shades work well together and with the furnishings you have chosen.

Not for the faint-hearted! In this scheme, the violet wall will appear to recede, the mustard wall to advance and the ceiling, despite being painted blue-green, is so much darker than the walls that it will dominate the room, lowering its apparent height.

Once you've knocked down walls, added windows and radiators and completed your electrical work, you should have the basic framework of your new-look room completed. Now all that remains is to put your colour theory and style research into practice and establish your decorating scheme.

You will probably have already been gathering inspiration while working on your basic preparations for the room, but don't rush into putting them into practice. Once your scheme actually begins to materialize, you may discover that it doesn't look quite as you imagined or that you would prefer something slightly different after all. That's why it is so important to take your time and plan your scheme theoretically on paper first, so that you can make any mistakes or change your mind as often as you like without wasting time and money on the real thing. By gathering a good collection of fabric and paint samples and creating a sample board just as a professional would, you can play around with ideas for as long as it takes for you to feel completely happy with the finished effect.

Gathering material

Before you can start to work on your sample board, you need to gather your materials. By now you should have got some idea of the sort of colour scheme you want in order to create the right look for your small room. The more cautious among you may have decided to go for light, cool shades in order to create a more spacious effect, but remember to check the sort of light your room receives first and go back to the chapter on colour theory if you are still unsure about your decision. Bear in mind too the rules of scale when you are decorating a small space: large patterns will dominate a small room and make the area seem even smaller, so it is wiser to stick to small-scale designs. Once you have decided on the sort of colour and effect you want to achieve, you can head to the shops and start to gather samples of fabrics, wallpapers, carpeting and paint.

Don't be too cautious or selective about what you gather at this stage. Collect as wide

Gathering samples of the fabrics you like the look of, then placing them in relation to the other elements of your scheme, is the only way to get an impression of how the finished room will look. When you are planning for a small room, large patterns such as many of these may be too overpowering for the scale of furniture or window they are dressing, but in a one-room apartment, where the proportions of the overall living space and windows may be larger, smaller patterns would be lost and look out of place.

a range of samples as you can so that you have plenty of ideas to play with when you get home. When asking for samples in shops, be as bold as you dare. Many retailers will try to get away with giving you only a small snippet of material or paper that will give you no idea of the complete pattern once you get home. Try to get larger samples or ask if you can borrow the sample book, but if you get nowhere, accept the fact that you may have to pay for a decent sized piece. The same goes for paint samples. Collect the small cards that display the various colours available by all means – they can give a good general guide to the choices available – but remember that a colour will never be perfectly reproduced by the printing process. You should always have a sample of the actual paint

before you buy half a dozen tins. Many of the main manufacturers produce small tester pots, which contain enough to cover about two square metres (yards), but if the brand you are drawn to is not available in tester size, you will have to buy the smallest available pot instead to try it out *in situ*.

The job of sample collecting will be much easier if you concentrate on only one room design at a time. It is all too easy to lose track of what you are looking for. Each room you are working on may be small, but it still has as many elements to consider as a larger space – carpets, curtains, walls and upholstery – so it needs to be taken just as seriously. Take your notebook or folder of measurements, from floor area for carpeting to wall area for wallpaper and window sizes for curtains and

Stripes and prints are a combination that never fails to please, and the cool blue and white are ideal for a small space. To prevent the overall effect from being too cold, or if they are destined for a room that receives little light, consider adding a dash of warm yellow or pink to the sample board.

The best samples are:

☐ Generously sized

☐ Can be moved around the room

☐ Labelled with details of price, manufacturer etc.

☐ In line with specifications for colour and pattern

☐ Affordable

☐ Suit the scale of your room

☐ As practical and hard-wearing as the room demands

blinds, with you when you shop and remember to take a calculator. You won't be ordering at this stage, but it means that you will be able to work out on the spot how much it would cost to use a particular range or design in your room and so decide whether you can afford to consider it at all.

Try not to be tempted by the coordinated ranges while you window shop. It is easy to opt for the wallpaper border, fabric and wallpaper that a manufacturer has already coordinated, but the final effect will be a lot less interesting, personal and successful than one you have put together yourself, even if doing so does take more time.

As you gather your samples, note down the manufacturer, design name and any reference number so that you have them to hand for ordering. It will be useful if you also note down the price, the name of the shop you found it in, the fabric width and pattern repeat so you can double check your sums when you get home, and this information will be invaluable if you have to replace anything at a later date. An adhesive label on the back of the fabric makes it easy and quick to refer to your notes.

Not many people can accurately carry colours in their head so, for as long as you are gathering new samples, carry around what you have already picked out in a transparent bag. It will help you make on the spot decisions about whether a new fabric is going to work with your plans.

The choice of fabrics available can be overwhelming at first, but once you have decided on your budget and colour scheme and have established the size of pattern that will work best in your room, the range open to you will be more limited. Heavy, textured fabrics such as these require a large window if they are to be shown to best effect, so if your windows are small, opt for samples in lighter, natural weaves.

White tiles will work with any colour and in any size of room, but do add a touch of warmth so that the room does not look like a hospital. Remember to consider scale when you are choosing tiles for walls or floors. Large white tiles with a small insert will work in most sizes of room, but large deep coloured tiles, even if combined with equally large white ones, will look out of proportion in a small space.

The colour you paint your walls is going to dictate the success (or otherwise) of the whole room, so a large area of your sample board should be coated with this paint. You may want to paint your board completely with the chosen colour and lay the other samples on top of it, so that you can be sure it will work with every element of the room.

It is always best to apply the paint you are considering directly to the wall in question so that you can assess how the colour works *in situ* and at different times of day when the room receives different degrees of light.

Home testing

Once you've gathered your samples, you will probably find that you eliminate some of them as soon as you get home. Seeing them away from the shop lights and actually in your room will often make quite a difference, but that is fine because you have saved yourself from making a costly mistake. Most design mistakes result from an inability to imagine what a particular wallpaper will look like once it is actually hanging on the wall, and how the curtains or bedspread will look sitting next to it. Playing with large samples of material actually in the room will give a far more accurate impression of what the final effect will be.

Fix your samples temporarily in the spaces they are intended for. Tack a length of wallpaper to the wall, or paint some lining paper or a large piece of white card with your sample of paint and do the same. This is a good opportunity to practise any paint effects you are thinking of trying and, if your walls are papered at the moment, gives a more accurate impression of how the colour will look on a plain wall, rather than over a shiny vinyl. You may need to put up several examples of wallpaper or paint, or move the one sample you have around the room so you can see how it looks under different lights. Put your carpet sample on the floor and attach your fabric samples to the sofa, armchair, window or wherever they will be in the final scheme. Keep them there for at least a week, noting how they look under natural and artificial light and at different times of day, especially the times that you use that particular living space the most. This should help you to discount certain samples and establish a few preferences.

Making a sample board

Once you have focused your ideas and have begun to come to some decisions, it is worth making a sample board so that you can get a good impression of how the various elements of the room will work together. A good design is well balanced – that is, every element of the room should work in unison with the rest, rather than making a grand impact of its own. Anyone walking into your newly designed interior should comment on how attractive or welcoming the whole effect is not on how dramatic your curtains are. A sample board will help you to achieve this, because it will allow you to play around with the various colours, patterns and textures, and at the same time to create an impression of the scale of the room and how the different elements will work when seen in the same proportions as they will eventually appear in reality.

Use a piece of white or suitably coloured card as the base for the board. It should be at least A4 (11¾ × 8¼in) in size. The finished board will not only be a useful design tool, it will become a good reference point and, who knows, maybe even a work of art – so you may want to take as much time and care over it as would a professional who was using it as a means of presenting the scheme to a client.

Before you start cutting up your fabric samples, consider their scale in relation to one another. The key to a successful board is to think of it as representing your complete room, or a corner of the room where all the furnishing samples come together, such as by a window. Try to picture which samples will command the greatest expanse of visible space. It will usually be the floor and walls, in which case the samples you are considering for those areas should take up the greatest proportion of space on the sample board.

It may be that you cannot get actual samples for your floor covering or that you are intending to have a natural wood flooring rather than carpeting. If this is the case, try to use something that will at least give an impression of the colour or texture of that covering on the board. You may want to stain or paint a piece of wood and include it on your board or use a piece of fabric or some paint to represent the shade of the flooring.

Once you have cut these samples to size,

Making a sample board will help you to avoid costly mistakes. You will get a good impression of the overall scheme if you cut samples roughly to the scale they will be seen in the finished room. Two wallpapers, separated by a dado rail, are being considered, and the fabric for the curtaining (top right) is positioned next to both. The striped fabric may be used for the upholstery, and the smaller squares indicate the possible colours for lampshades, cushions and so on. The floor covering (bottom left) takes a proportionately large area of the board.

consider the samples for the next largest items in the room – often your sofa material and your curtains. Pinking shears will give an attractive edge to the materials you cut, which will improve the overall presentation of your board, or you may prefer to cut a curtain fabric in such a way that allows you to fold the fabric as the curtains might fall – you could even make a representative little tie-back for artistic effect. Next think about the fabrics you are considering for smaller items, such as cushions and lampshades, and include them on the board, cutting them in proportion to the other pieces.

Play around with the samples of fabric as they would appear in the room, placing them adjacent to and overlapping one another, until you have built up a picture of how the interior

All systems go

Once you've firmly established the samples you are going to use in your scheme, you can go ahead and make your purchases. However, before you place an order you should always check the following:

☐ Have you allowed enough for pattern repeats?

☐ Are the fabrics suitable for your purposes – curtains, upholstery and so on?

☐ Do they meet fire-retarding regulations?

☐ How washable are the fabrics? Can they be dry cleaned?

☐ Are all your wallpaper rolls of the same batch number?

☐ Order a spare roll for future patchingup.

☐ Will the company accept unopened rolls of wallpaper or pots of paint for return?

could look. Don't be afraid to give yourself options even on the board however. Samples of fabric can be laid on top of one another and only fixed at the top so that you can lift back the various layers to give alternative looks.

Once the board is finished, judge it as critically as you can. Does it look as you wanted or expected it to? Is there a good balance of pattern and texture? Does the wallpaper, the carpet or the curtain fabric appear to be too dominant? Play around with the samples again if necessary, taking some out and putting others in, until you're happy with the overall look. Only when you are completely happy with the combinations, need you fix them on the board, butting them up close together so that you can't see the board below.

If you like, you can take your board even one step further and create what is sometimes referred to as a story board – that is, a sample board that gives a more complete picture of your design work. Such a board may include space for a small-scale plan of the room (see Chapter 1), any magazine cuttings that are the inspiration behind the new look and even cuttings from catalogues to illustrate your choice of furniture and fittings. These boards are very practical reference points, so it is best if you limit it to a size that you can carry with you when you are looking for further materials for the room or consulting decorators.

So that's it. You've designed the first scheme for your home. All you need to do now is sign a few cheques and start decorating. Perhaps the hard work has only just begun after all!

When you are considering fabric samples, try to look at the whole pattern so that every colour and aspect of the design can be considered. The large, plump fruit of this fabric may be overpowering for a small room, and if you were to take home a sample that showed only the small floral area of the design, the other elements of the scheme would be out of proportion.

Index

Picture acknowledgements

All pictures courtesy of Elizabeth Whiting and Associates

Tim Beddow 31, 39, 126; Jean-Paul Bonhommet 4, 48, 72–3, 75, 83, 117, 131, 143; Nick Carter 91; Nick Carter/Amanda Baird 61; Nick Carter/Andrew Blatt 40; Michael Crockett 153; Michael Dunne 53, 57, 60, 79, 104, 132, 139, 146, 149; Michael Dunne/John Wright 76–7; Andreas von Einsiedel 7, 8, 32, 58, 87, 93, 110; Andreas von Einsiedel/Anaya/Elizabeth Whiting and Associates 96; Andreas von Einsiedel/Andre De Caqueray 6; Andreas von Einsiedel/Christian Stocker 129; Brian Harrison 15, 100; Brian Harrison/Ilsley 86; Brian Harrison/Jane Meakin 45; Brian Harrison/Judi Goodwin 107; Brian Harrison/Gosman 124; Huntley Hedworth 20; Graham Henderson 9, 89; Rodney Hyett 13, 18, 22, 33, 37, 90, 94, 103, 106, 108, 115, 144; Andrew Kolesnikow 92; Tom Leighton 31, 69, 112; Tom Leighton/Jenny Armit 29; Tom Leighton/Charles Rutherford 44, 65, 80; Tom Leighton/Virginia Wolf 98; Di Lewis 46, 54, 102; Di Lewis/Buston 125; Di Lewis/Caroline Green 84; Neil Lorimer 1, 10, 88, 121, 151; Neil Lorimer/Paul Kelly 17; Mark Luscombe-Whyte 122; Nadia MacKenzie 49, 63, 105, 152, 154; Ian Parry 150; Spike Powell 21, 26, 36, 50–1, 59, 111, 114, 118, 138; Spike Powell/James and Linda Fenwick 16; Spike Powell/Heike Martin 148; Dennis Stone 19, 120; Dennis Stone/Jill Visser 66; Tim Street Porter 137, 155; Friedhelm Thomas 71, 123; Jerry Tubby 130; Simon Upton 2, 28, 42–3, 70, 78, 135; Elizabeth Whiting and Associates 30, 109, 134, 154–5, 157; Peter Woloszynski 62; Shona Wood 140, 145; Cathy Yuan/Carol Yuan 56.